Come Back:

How Past Lives with Animals Changed the Way I Think about Death

*For –
Diana Thomas*

Tina Proffitt

*All my best!
Tina Proffitt*

Copyright 2017
All rights reserved.

Come Back

To my gorgeous husband—my hero
and inspiration for the hero in every romance novel
I've written.
I could never live without your love—I love you
Always!

Names of people and some animals have been changed to protect anonymity except when used by permission.

Tina Proffitt

Table of Contents

Preface

Introduction: The Day I Almost Killed Myself   11

1. Wally's Story: Painful Longing   15
2. Holly's Story: Port in the Storm   21
3. Mitten's Story: Baby-doll   26
4. Epona's Story: Got Your Back   32
5. George's Story: When No One Else Did   41
6. Harley's Story: My Hero   49
7. Brittney's Story: Unrequited Love   58
8. Todd's Story: Letting Go   65
9. Kitty's Story: I Love You to Death   73
10. Puss in Boots' Story: Hungry Heart   81
11. Petey's Story: 911   86
12. Duke's Story: One Night Stand   94
13. Juliet's Story: Stobs   99
14. Daisy, Scotch, and Roger's Story: Neighbors and Friends   109
15. Susan's Story: Mirror, Mirror   118

Conclusion: What I've Learned Along the Way   127

Do It Yourself Communication   140

Suggested Reading and Listening

About the Author

Come Back

Preface

From the time I was old enough to speak, my mother taught me that one day, we would all live in Heaven together. Sounded good. "Gramma Jackie and Grady, Grandma and Grandpa, aunts, uncles, all my cousins, even our dogs and cats we'd buried would be there," she said.

I thought it was wonderful that I didn't have to say goodbye to my loved ones *forever; I* just had to wait a while to be reunited. But there was a caveat, something I had to do to get myself a ticket to Heaven and then once I was there, I would never leave.

That didn't sound so hot to me. A place I could never leave?

"But it will be so wonderful, you'll never want to," my mother said.

And you would be there, and we would be together forever?

It was this notion of forever with people I wasn't always fond of; my heart wasn't so sure I wanted to be with them forever.

Forever made my palms sweaty.

To this day, my mind cannot comprehend eternity. And admittedly just the thought still makes me a little uneasy.

According to her, the first few times she asked me (a toddler) to ask Jesus to live in my heart to avoid going to Hell with the Devil forever, I said, *no.*

No was one of those words that got me into a lot of trouble. For as far back as I can remember, before my conscious memory, until I was fifteen, my parents punished me for everything from talking back to what they laughingly referred to as *GP* or *general purposes*, meaning that if I didn't need a whipping at the time, they'd probably missed one. To this day, the sound of my husband taking off his belt in our bedroom makes me cringe.

All those years I was told that God was my Heavenly Father and that he loved me and had a special plan for my life. But none of my questions were answered. What am I doing here if Heaven is the goal? Why does my life hurt so much? Where do children go when they die if they didn't have a chance to ask Jesus into their hearts? If God loves me, why did he create a place called Hell for me to burn for eternity in case I didn't do exactly what he asked me to do?

It was the first day of classes at Greenville Technical College my sophomore year. At the end of class, my English 201 professor, and retired U.S. sailor, got our attention with his booming voice for his parting words. "I've given you my syllabus," he said, sitting at his desk. "You know what I expect from you, what papers to turn in, and when. I'm not going to hover over you and remind you when you've got a paper due. That's not my job." Then he smiled, like an evil villain. "I've given you just enough rope. By the end of the semester, we'll see which ones of you run with it and which ones of you hang yourselves with it."

I see a parallel here between his words and what I was told about God. I was taught that God gave us free will to live our lives as we choose. But that if we did not make the right choice, we would suffer for eternity. If we made the right one however, we would live forever in peace. No pressure. From what I could tell, that meant that, like my professor, God also gave me just enough leash, or rope as it were, to run free or to hang myself with. That didn't make sense to me. What loving parent or God would do that to their children?

As I grew and had children of my own, finding answers to my questions became more and more pressing. Instead of trying to avoid them as I had in my youth, I focused on them, trying to find answers that would resonate within me. My search led me to agree with my parents on one important aspect, that our souls never die. We are continuous, therefore our relationships can be also, if we want them to be. The main difference I have with my upbringing is that we can leave *Heaven* and come back to Earth to do it all over again.

When I finally reached this answer that made sense to me, after my initial shock, I experienced a moment of "Yes! That's it!" And what followed was "peace that passeth understanding".

My path has led me to many wonderful teachers. And through my study, I have found that understanding why I am here can be as simple as looking to the animals around me. Reflected in their eyes, particularly the furry-faced ones, are the souls that have also lived many lifetimes. Because animals are simple, that is not to say simple-minded, but pure and authentic, they can help me find the answers I seek.

As animals, they live much shorter lives than we humans and much less complicated ones. They do not carry emotional baggage like we do. They eat, sleep, and love. And it is because of this simplicity that they grasp the truth of living. And most importantly, they are here for a reason just as we are. And since they have chosen to live their lives with us, and we them, it comes as no surprise that we are part of that choice for a reason.

Why do our animal companions burst into our lives, love us faster, stronger, cleaner than any other soul, then leave us before we're ready?

I ask myself that question everyday as I look at my Bernese Mountain Dog, Juliet. I don't really have an answer that truly satisfies. She is here to love me unconditionally. Then why, I ask, can't she do that for fifty or sixty years instead of ten? She is here to teach me to love unconditionally. Then the same question pops up.

Sugar, a dog who lived a much shorter life than most, springs to my mind. My family had moved to Greenwood, South Carolina and adopted her, a six month old mixed English Bulldog pup.

One Saturday morning, I played in the brick carport of a neighbor friend. We were both around six years old. The whole day ahead of us, Katie and I braided our doll's hair, unaware that my family's dog had just been hit by a car about a hundred yards away. In the days before leash laws, dogs ran around our neighborhood from yard to yard, greeting their own dog-friends and fighting with others. This day, Sugar and Pumpkin, another neighbor's dog, ran together. Unfortunately, they crossed the street at the bottom of a rather steep hill. The car's driver never saw her coming.

Pumpkin rocketed up the hill towards my friend's house, barking at us furiously. She would run back down the hill the way she'd come, then back up, returning to us, barking all the way.

"I think she wants us to follow her," my friend,

Come Back

Katie, said.

I agreed, and follow her we did. At the bottom of the hill, my friend and I found Sugar. She lay there on the road, unconscious. Her eyes closed, she was most likely already dead. I remember a fly walked across her closed eyes.

Katie looked up at me from beneath her feathered bangs. "She'll be okay," she said. Her mother was a nurse, and Katie, a kind soul, had her mother's bed-side manner.

But it was evident to me even at such a young age, that Sugar would not be okay. The brown-eyed bundle of energy that we called Sugar was gone.

The young woman whose car had struck Sugar had gotten out. She wore a dress and heels. I'll never forget seeing her cry for my dog, apologizing over and over again. It had a profound effect on me. My six-year-old heart went out to her. I wasn't the only person affected by this tragedy. She would never forget that day either, an accident that ended a life.

If the purpose of our animal companion's lives (here I'll refer to domesticated, but if you're lucky enough to love farm animals, insert them) is to teach us something that we otherwise couldn't learn from any other soul, then why can't they stick around a little longer? Why do we fall so hard so fast only to have it end in inevitable, soul-crushing heartbreak?

There is one answer I have found that gives me a little peace and it is this: it's not about us.

By this I mean, the purpose of our animal companion's lives isn't all about us, the "owner". It's about them.

Sugar's reasons for coming here to Earth, spending

a short few months with my family, then leaving, were her own. They were for her soul's growth and we got the benefit of loving her for a brief time.

As Father Brown, the great fictional character written by G.K. Chesterton, once said, "This is not farewell but a brief interlude before we meet again."

Anyone who's looked into the eyes of a Bernese Mountain Dog, a Labrador Retriever, a Dalmatian, just to name a few, doesn't have to wonder if there's a soul inside looking back. We know it. And what's even better, they've got something to say to us if we'll learn to listen. And that listening is something each and every one of us can do.

Our animal friends are with us for a reason. They chose us for a reason. All souls are infinite. Like all of us, they can take on the form of whatever body they choose. Their souls chose dog, cat, or horse, and then chose to take up residence with us, the humans, the two-legged souls. And they do teach us. They teach us an immeasurable amount about love, respect, boundaries, forgiveness, and unconditional love. But that's just the things we get from them. They are here on Earth for *their* soul's growth just as we are. Granted they've chosen a body that doesn't stick around for the long haul. But that's exactly what they had in mind when they chose it.

As I write, I live with a beautiful Bernese Mountain Dog, Juliet. I knew going in that I would only get eight years with her. If I was lucky, ten. But knowing that at the outset didn't and doesn't make me stop hoping that somehow she will miraculously become the longest living Bernese ever in recorded history. No, it doesn't. I still haven't stopped hoping.

Come Back

But the rational part of me ticks off the passing of each birthday like a clock. She just celebrated her seventh year in September.

In the same way we choose our families, friends, co-workers, and neighbors in order to work out whatever unfinished business from the past we have with those people, so it is the same with our animal friends. And vice versa, they are here to work out theirs with us. The undercurrents of our relationships may run so deep that we may never become consciously aware of them. But at some level, we know why they are here. And more importantly, *they* know why they are here.

In the final chapter of this book, I will share with you my method for communicating with the animals whose stories you are about to read, some living and some dead.

This book is not meant as a guide or a treatise on the topic of reincarnation. It is not meant to convince or persuade anyone on its subject matter. It is simply a collection of essays taken from my life. I came to my spiritual beliefs as we all do I think—to find a way of coping, a way of believing that ignites our passion or at the very least doesn't leave us unsettled or unfulfilled. The promise that this life is not all there is, is a comforting concept to me. I like knowing that my loved ones will be with me again—that goodbye is never really goodbye, but farewell, until we meet again.

Tina Proffitt
October 31, 2016

Tina Proffitt

Introduction

Come Back

The Day I Almost Killed Myself

I'll never forget that Monday morning almost exactly four years ago today, the day I almost killed myself in front of my children.

I stood in front of Richland Creek Animal Hospital. The dark brown building fronts a six-lane highway. In my heather green t-shirt, blue jeans, and tennis shoes, my hair pulled back into a ponytail, less than ten feet from my back, cars whizzed past, their slipstream literally blowing my hair. The sun sparkled off the river rock gray of my Landcruiser's back door. In the narrow parking lot from the corner of my eye, I became faintly aware of a woman decked out in heels and dress who had just stepped out of her car parked beside mine.

The time of year was the same as I now write, November. The trees had dropped their leaves. And the grass had withered bare and brown. Each day, full dark arrived before dinnertime. Thanksgiving loomed on the horizon. I thought of all the things I needed to accomplish before the end of that day: lunch as soon as we got back home, homeschool lessons, dinner in the slow-cooker, Juliet's new prescription for antibiotics. My work-out for the day suddenly disappeared from my to-do list.

I closed the back of my truck, Juliet and my kids tucked safely inside. Instead of having already completed our Math, Science, English, and Social Studies lessons that morning, we were in the next town at the veterinarian clinic. We had made an impromptu trip that morning. Juliet had had a bad reaction to a flea bite over the weekend and had taken it out on her entire hip. As a result, she now wore the e-collar of shame. Not to mention, she had received a naughty sticker on the doctor's chart for trying to nip the assistant who'd shaved her raw skin.

As I rounded the truck to my door, out of nowhere the woman in heels sprawled onto the pavement, falling face first to the ground. She did not get back up. And to my horror, she lost her hold of the leash that had been in her hand. Her little brown dog hurtled itself across the dangerous road in a blind panic.

My first thought—*What if that were Juliet running away?* What would I do? With every fiber of my being I knew I would be lost without her, wondering where she was, hurting inside, missing her, worrying about her. I couldn't stand by and just watch.

"Stay here!" I ordered my children, who by now wore their seat belts. I pushed the key lock for the doors, locking them inside the truck.

I knew what I had to do, and I didn't think twice. I acted on pure adrenaline.

Now, I'm by no means an athlete. The peak of physical dexterity for me has always been aerobic videos. (I brought home straight A report cards while my siblings brought home trophies.) But I can run pretty fast.

The next few minutes whizzed by at a blur. My feet touched pavement without considering the consequences. The curve at the top of the road to my right loomed over me, a menacing giant laughing at me. If I could just make it across before a car burst around its hidden corner, I'd be okay.

I'm still not completely comfortable with the choice I made that day. The memory of how close I

Come Back

came to those cars has the power to make me wince.

How could I have done such an irresponsible thing?

That's exactly what I wanted to know. It had been just a stranger's dog, my rational mind tried to convince me. But I couldn't accept its words. Somehow I knew better.

In the next few pages, I will attempt to paint an accurate picture of events leading up to that day—how my love for animals landed me in this predicament in the first place. And how I learned through the animals that second chances don't just come to the positively contrite or the deserving few. Second chances are gifts from the universe. No one has to be good enough or grateful enough to receive gifts. We just get them. We all get second and even third chances. And what's more—we all deserve them.

Tina Proffitt

1.
Wally's Story

Come Back

Painful Longing

"Let's go get a Coke out of the garage!"

"I don't think we should," I said, young, but still old enough to know better.

"Come on!" Dawn said. "Nobody will see."

Dawn, my friend and playmate, who lived across the street, had been right. Of her two much older siblings and one younger, not a one of them had noticed us sneaking into the garage that day, none except for her dog.

Wally, her aging Dachshund, waddled out to join us. Our three-year-old hands wrapped around pilfered bottles of Coke, we laughed and giggled as he looked up at us expectantly. Dawn stood in front of the old refrigerator in that stuffy garage that day, the dog between us, my back against a cabinet full of hunting supplies. When we'd finished our drinks, it was decided that we could then return to our play outdoors. The year was 1978, and the summer humidity of Florida could at times be unbearable. This was one of those days.

"Let's take Wally out with us," Dawn said.

She leaned over to wrap her little arms around his middle.

"He doesn't want to be picked up," I said, knowing these were the words the dog would speak if he could.

"He won't mind."

As Dawn stood, barely balancing the straining dog between us, I felt as if I stared down the barrel of a loaded shotgun. Tiny teeth bared, he was pointed right at me. It was all over before I knew what had happened. My left cheek ached all of a sudden. My left hand and thumb stung.

As I headed for home, I looked down at the red streaks on my left hand. I crossed the street back to my house. My blood pooled on tender flesh as the heat from the black asphalt street burned through the bottoms of my sandals.

In an instant, my outlook on animals was forever changed. My scars became a constant reminder of that day. To this day, I can still recall the sound of his growls and see his angry face.

Fast forward twenty-three years and I was the mother of a toddler. We lived next door to a Dachshund who used her front yard to do her business.

At the time, my son enjoyed playing in our front yard. That was where all the action lived: cars whizzing by, a swing hanging from our big oak tree, a garden hose for spraying plants and people who weren't looking, all the things the back yard lacked.

Often times, our play time and Maggie's bathroom time coincided. I was always happy to see my neighbor, but lately, I'd begun to feel a nagging sense of foreboding when the dog came out. She would always bound towards us, barking, as was her right of course. This was after all, her home too, and she let us know that—one of those boundary lessons I would get again and again. But every time she did this, I would make a bee line for my son, scoop him up, and hold him tight until Maggie went back inside.

One day, I explained to my very understanding neighbor that her dog scared me because as a small child I had been bitten by a Dachshund. After the words were out of my mouth however, I began to question their validity.

Was I really afraid of Dachshunds? Was that even possible?

I thought about those questions for the rest of that day. A week went by before we saw Maggie again. During that time, I had decided it was silly for me to fear a dog that could at best nip my ankles. And I certainly didn't want to teach my son to fear dogs. So the next time she headed for us, instead of scooping my son off his feet, I squatted down, positioning myself between him and Maggie and greeted her. And to my great relief, she stopped barking, looked at us, then went off to do her business. From then on, I made a habit of saying hello to Maggie. I wouldn't say we ever bonded, but we had reached a truce. The bounding and barking seemed to become tiresome to her, and after a while she stopped entirely, ignoring us instead.

Wally biting me that day so many years before suddenly became a great lesson for me. Although I didn't realize it at only three years old, I had been able to "hear" him speak. It was a natural ability that I had incarnated with. Wally had *told* Dawn not to pick him up, but she hadn't listened. And unfortunately, his sharp end had been pointed at me.

Ultimately, I had a choice. I could let the memory of that day teach me or I could let it paralyze me. I chose the former. And I hadn't been the only one with lessons to learn.

Wally's story started centuries before that day in that hot Florida garage.

As a monk, living in a monastery in Florida, he used a blade to shave the top of his hair every morning before services began. He donned his brown robe cinched around his bulging waist with a rope.

As a young man, he had never known what it was like to be with a woman. He knew from the start of his life that he would one day take vows. He felt great pride in his devotion. But he never shook his desire to be with a woman.

At the end of each day, in the waning light of his room, he picked up his leather whip. Removing his robe, his back and chest bare, he lashed himself. One lash for every time he'd thought of a woman's body that day. Sometimes ten, sometimes fifteen, while baking bread, or singing, or praying, his thoughts intruded. Ridding himself of his flesh was easier than the very natural, innate, human sexual desire he felt. The constant pain was his reminder to remain pure, to remain chaste. Even the slightest brush or touch could send his body into painful spasms. Happiest when he was alone, he kept to his room much of the time, never venturing far from his home.

In his most recent incarnation as a Dachshund, Wally experienced considerable back pain as well. Only this pain began when he was struck by a car. His back hurt him terribly from that time on. And being picked up by my friend that day must have been excruciating for him. His warning growls had gone ignored. Who wouldn't lash out?

But instead of living isolated as a monk as he had been in his former incarnation, Wally found himself this time around in the company of a large, sometimes boisterous family who loved him very much. In fact, the family owned two Dachshunds, Wally and a female Dachshund named Wanda. In choosing to reincarnate

Come Back

into this family, he had healed that part of himself that had been so lonely in his previous existence.

Wally did not live much longer after that day. He was run over by a garbage truck and died instantly. His back pain was over.

Since the realization that I could commune with animals if I chose to, my interest was kindled. Wally biting me became an important lesson just as Maggie living next door to me enabled me to realize that lesson. I could then see and recognize that previously dormant desire inside me to commune with the animals.

Anytime I want, I can look in the mirror and see three hair-like scars running the length of my left cheek or look down at my left thumb and see the scars on my thumb and hand. Wally had beautifully fulfilled his purpose in my life, showing me that animals and humans can understand one another—by biting me on my face.

Tina Proffitt

2.
Holly's Story

Come Back

me and Holly

Port in the Storm

Taking a small step back in time, there was Holly.

When I think of Pensacola, Florida, it's impossible for me not to think of hurricanes. We had several of them in the five years I lived there, candles burning, power out, a big deal to a little kid.

Holly, a Dalmatian, white with liver spots, was according to my mother, *my* dog.

Although I don't remember much of my time with Holly, I was twenty-two months old when she was two months old, the same age as my new baby sister. There are pictures of me with her. One is of me, wearing a navy blue snow suit and a huge smile on my little face, as Holly pranced around me in the backyard. Snow fell around us. Yes, in Florida. The second picture is of me a year or two later. My long, brown hair sprawled out around me. It was the middle of the day. Sun poured in from the front window, but I still wore my pajamas. I'm sure that this was one of those days when I had been sick. I suffered from persistent congestion (all the unshed tears). I was asleep with my head on a pillow on the living room floor. Holly slept right beside me. And the third is of the two of us even older together in her pin in the back yard where according to my mother, I spent a lot of time.

And although my conscious memory of Holly is sketchy (my most vivid memory is of the farm where we left her before moving to Greenwood, South Carolina) my soul remembers. The Greek word philosophy comes from the root words meaning *to love with wisdom*. And that was precisely Holly's purpose in coming here.

Holly's soul had at one time been my father who had loved me with his whole heart. Our time together as girl and dog brought my soul the much needed love and acceptance I had received from him in that previous life.

Because of my parents' belief that not sparing the rod would ensure bringing me up right, I learned from a very young age that I needed to be *good*. One of my mother's favorite musings is the way I used to mispronounce a sentence I'd learned from her constant repetition. "Has my 'havior proved?" I used to ask her, meaning that whatever I wanted to do: play outside, watch cartoons, have a popsicle, all depended on whether or not my *behavior* had *improved*.

Come Back

Because of honest adult conversations and my years in psychotherapy, we today enjoy a mutually loving relationship. If my parents could do it all over again tomorrow, I believe they would do things differently. But what if their regret isn't necessary? What if they did and acted in the way that was necessary for me to grow? In other words, I needed to go through the separation and self-doubt. Just as Holly needed to be my source of comfort—my parents needed to be the source of my pain—in order for my soul to grow.

In this life, at a time when I would desperately need it, Holly was there for me to show me the unconditional love I did not receive from my parents. And although I cannot recall any particular events involving Holly, there is a warm fuzziness I feel when I think of her. I know she loved me.

Holly and I also came together to forgive. Before our incarnation as little girl and dog, in yet another incarnation, I had been Holly's mother.

The two of us had shared a strong bond that needed to be healed. As her mother, I had abandoned her. Her soul had been my son at the time. When he had needed me, I hadn't been there for him. I had not had the resources to care for him. A poor woman without a husband to care for the two of us, I left my son at an orphanage. The little boy Holly's soul had been had not survived. He was left alone, neglected by the caregivers there. He had died in that orphanage.

Leaving Holly at the farm in this life became a repetition of that abandonment. Holly had loved me unconditionally as a child loves his parent, and I, a powerless child myself, had been forced to leave her.

This time, however, the results were not disastrous for her. She was not sent to an orphanage but went to live on a big farm where she could run (her favorite pastime). She lived there for the rest of her days, happy and free. Holly was able to forgive me this time because she could see how powerless I was, as I had been in our previous life, unable to make the choice to keep her.

While I'll never forget those storms in Pensacola, I will always remember the unconditional love I received from Holly. I didn't have to be good enough; I didn't have to be anything except the innocent child I was.

Holly had been able to love me through a very difficult time in my childhood, which also made her better able to forgive me for my previous abandonment of her. When we can see the suffering of another, we are always better able to forgive. As Henry Wadsworth Longfellow wrote, "If we could read the secret history of our enemies, we should find in each man's life sorrow and suffering enough to disarm all hostility." It's the times when we can't see the suffering someone else is experiencing that makes life difficult, but since we're all human, we can assume they're suffering just as we are.

Come Back

3.
Mitten's Story

Tina Proffitt

Mittens

Baby-doll

We had moved again, the third time in as many years, this time from Greenwood, South Carolina to Decatur, Alabama. I was seven years old, the age by which we, all of us, have forgotten our previous existences and our purpose in coming here. My mother had just recovered from a severe depression during which she remained in bed much of the time. By moving, our family would *start over* again.

On this summer day, my mother drove me and my sister to the animal shelter. I don't recall all of the details of the trip, just the euphoria that pounded through me. I picked up that tiny meowing kitten and knew she was all mine. I became a mommy to a kitten that day. On the drive home in the back seat of our white station wagon, I couldn't stop gushing over her.

Look how big her green eyes are! They look so big in her tiny head! Look how big her ears look on her tiny body! Did you hear that squeak she just made? Feel how soft her fur is. She smells so good. Oh, look, she's trying to catch my hair between her little paws!

I named her Mittens.

A brown and black tabby became my dress-up doll. I even tucked her into an umbrella stroller (pictured) and we'd go for walks.

She tolerated me. She let me hold her on the porch swing and pose her for silly pictures. I loved playing with dolls at that age. I had two "adoption dolls" I loved, but nothing compared to pretending that Mittens was my baby. I learned that sometimes babies don't like to be babied. I learned the limits of an animal's patience (warning growls when I dressed her). But I loved every minute with her. Mittens taught me early on how *to love with wisdom.*

One of my fondest memories is of sitting on the back porch swing with her in my lap. Today, I have a back porch swing where my daughter and I are fond of swinging together, and I sometimes think of Mittens.

This wasn't the first life Mittens and I had enjoyed together.

It was late eighteenth century. Mittens' soul and mine lived in what today is called California. In that incarnation, I was her mother and we were very close. I taught her to make her own clothes. She and I would sit together, bone needles and animal hides in hand, sewing dresses together. We also loved to cook together. I taught her the things that my mother had taught me, and together over an open fire we made the meals for our family.

In many ways, our coming together as cat and girl in this life became a reunion of happy souls. We enjoyed ourselves then and we enjoyed ourselves in this life.

As my cat, she allowed me to reconnect with that part of my soul that recalled being her mother, enjoyed being her mother. Allowing me to nurture her helped me to heal that part of my heart that hurt, that needed to connect with a loving mother. Because our connections can remain with us forever, our soul never forgets how it feels to be loved even when we don't feel loved, and it remembers how it feels to be nurtured even when we don't feel nurtured. In other words, I knew something was missing even if I couldn't put a finger on it. The longing was there even though I had not experienced it in my current incarnation.

Mittens traveled with me and my family to Austin, Texas three years later where she remained a part of my heart through my turbulent teenage years. Unfortunately, she was not allowed to come with us to Greenville, South Carolina when we moved again seven years later. After a decade together, at seventeen years old, I had to say goodbye to her. She went to live with my best friend, Charity, and I never saw her again.

For Mittens, being left behind in Texas was a repetition of her mother's death. As a member of our previous family, her soul had not married, and so, when I, her mother, died, she felt abandoned. She had spent her life devoted to me, and my leaving her behind in Texas repeated that abandonment, that death.

As a girl, living totally dependent on my parents, I was unable to have a say in whether or not Mittens came with us when we moved. None of our four cats were allowed to move with us. Mittens was once again left behind alone.

The good news is that Mittens' soul is my daughter once more only this time, my human daughter. And just like our incarnation as Early American mother and daughter in California, today we enjoy the same love of baking together and making clothes together. Both skills incarnated with my daughter: a strong interest in cooking early on and a talent in clothes-making, sitting in her room as a young girl with needle and thread making clothes for her Barbie dolls.

And as I mentioned earlier that Mittens "tolerated" my dressing her up, the same could be said of my daughter now. As a two-year-old, her first "No!" to me was the dress I had picked out for her to wear. I celebrated that *No!* something I'd never been allowed to say to my parents. And from that day on, she picked out her own clothes. On many occasions, I was accompanied to the grocery store by a miniature princess in pink heels and tiara. It was important to her, so it was important.

She was a part of my life when I was just a girl, to love me and to be loved for those precious few years, at a time when I desperately wanted to nurture. Now our souls have reunited again. I have my daughter with me again, to love, to teach, to nurture her soul as she does mine.

Had I been able to look into Mittens' eyes then as a

girl and know that she and I were together for a very special purpose, that the soul of my daughter from lifetimes ago would return to me again to become my current daughter, I wonder how differently I could have viewed my life. Instead of seeing only the pain and longing, perhaps I could have felt the love that surrounded me, the love that waited for me. But then again, if I had known, perhaps that would have defeated the purpose.

Although I was not consciously aware of our history at the time, even for a few short, yet formative years, reconnecting with her soul housed in a cat's body allowed me to reconnect with a joyful part of my soul's history. And she was able to re-experience our connection as well.

Some reunions are simply happy ones even if they are altogether too brief.

Come Back

4.
Epona's Story

Tina Proffitt

Got Your Back

It was 1987, and my family and I lived in Texas. That summer we vacationed in the mountains of North Carolina where my maternal grandmother had spent her entire life. We had decided to spend the afternoon horseback riding, something we had all done as a family before. As we were the only ones there at the stables to ride that day, my father, mother, brother, sister, and I set out with our guide on horseback. I had never feared horses before that day. And I don't know that I do now, since I haven't ridden in so many decades. But nevertheless, we set out.

It was a fine day, cool but not cold. In the mountains, the weather can stay relatively cool even in the middle of summer. That day I wore long slacks (jeans were never permitted by the private schools my siblings and I attended, so I didn't own any) a short sleeve cotton blouse with horizontal pastel stripes, and a thrift store pair of cowgirl boots that my grandmother had given to me. I was the only one of my family members to wear boots that day. Despite the taunts I received from my brother for wearing boots too big for my feet, I was shortly to become very grateful I had chosen to wear them.

We set off into the cool shade of the woods. The ground beneath our horse's feet was dark, soft earth. The trees and plants were blooming in the shade of the woods, reaching for little droplets of sunlight. To this day, I love learning about the herbs that have been used for centuries to heal, and I incorporate them into mine and my family's health regime. Reading about these magical, God-given plants makes me feel connected to a time in my lives that has long past, a time of simple living, a time of listening to my intuition and gleaning from Mother Earth all the healing she has to offer our human bodies. One of my favorite forms of learning about the past is through historical fiction novels, but I also love biographies. Whenever I read about people from the past, my writer's brain kicks in and I begin to imagine all sorts of details surrounding that person's life, sometimes even getting a very real sense that I have heard of them before—maybe even knew them.

That day our gentle path wound around the mountain and would take about an hour to traverse. The path narrowed and our horses out of habit fell into a single file. Our guide was in front, followed by my father, my brother behind him, my mother, my sister, and I brought up the rear. And like a good cowgirl, I had my hands on the reins and my boots securely in the stirrups. The horses had taken this path so many times, they could have done it without the guide. But this day would prove different from all the others.

Yellow jackets, as most are aware, make their nests in the ground. Every horse in that line managed to avoid the nest on the path that day, every horse except mine. My horse, Epona, stopped suddenly, then took off at a tear past the line of horses in front of us, even past the guide. I can still feel the power of the horse's body beneath me as I held on for dear life. I had not seen or heard the yellow jackets, but my horse had. I was oblivious of the danger, but my horse was keenly aware.

Here is where I will remind you that we were on a mountain. North Carolina has some spectacular mountains and even more beautiful vistas from the tops of those mountains. You can see for miles when you're atop of one of those blue giants. And because of this spectacular scenery, if you step to the edge of one of these mountain paths like the one we were on that day, you can see for miles. In parts, you can also see straight down. And my horse was headed straight for one of those parts.

Our guide screamed at my horse to stop. I screamed too, although nothing in particular. I could also hear my parents yelling my name. The edge of the mountain loomed closer and closer in my vision. I tugged as hard as I could on the reins. I braced my feet in the stirrups, pushing against them. Nothing stopped this horse. Then, lo and behold, as if he had brakes on his shoes, before we reached the edge, Epona stopped.

We all got off of our horses, holding onto the reins, and caught our collective breath. I was particularly grateful to feel the ground beneath my boots once more. The six of us agreed that the smartest thing to do would be to head back to the stables. And as my whole body still shook, I had no problem with that.

By the time we reached the bottom of the mountain, the horses had calmed back down and the humans had as well. And although I don't remember which one of us suggested it (not me though), it was decided that I should get back on my horse—you know, to prove to me that horses were safe.

I have since decided that the meaning of the proverb, *when you fall off your horse, get back up,* should only be taken figuratively, never literally. It's great advice. Don't let setbacks keep you from pursuing your dreams. Perseverance and determination, after all, pave the road to success. But when you fall off a real horse, for whatever reason, I can't think of a good reason to get back on. Besides the horse must have had reasons of his own.

Now, I wish I could say the story ends here. We all ride down the mountain, say goodbye, happy ending. But I can't.

We could try it again. Let's go back up the mountain.

Sure. We've got nothing to fear.

We headed back up the mountain.

This time however, the horse saw this one coming. We never got anywhere near the place in the path where he'd stepped on the yellow jackets' nest. He bolted long before that.

And I found myself once again on the back of a runaway horse. Once again, I screamed at the top of my twelve-year old lungs. This time, a small branch hanging from a tree poked the back of my throat, scratching my cheek on its way in.

Fortunately, the trail guide had had the foresight to stick close beside me. As the horse bolted, he grabbed hold of the reins in the nick of time. So the ride was much shorter this time, terrifying, but shorter.

And once again, our group found itself at the bottom of the mountain, staring at one another in a collective state of shock and disbelief.

When I complained that I tasted blood and why, my brother said, "If you hadn't had your big mouth open screaming, that wouldn't have happened."

I had become used to his verbal taunts by then. We'd had twelve years together as brother and sister. And he, five years old when I came along, had not forgiven me for being born. I had a refrain I repeated to myself in an attempt to protect myself whenever he humiliated me like this. *He can't hurt me.* Each time I repeated my refrain, I added another brick to the wall between us. But each time I did this, closing myself off from him, I unknowingly shut everyone out else as well. I wouldn't unlearn this behavior for many years, decades, to come. Through writing, I have become much more aware of the things I need to forgive.

No one spoke again the second time back to the stables. We dismounted and our guide collected our horses. Once they were all put away and enjoying hay, our guide grabbed a whip and thrashed my horse's back.

My mother flew into an instant rage. She yelled at the man to stop, rushing up behind the horse.

In fear, the horse kicked out behind himself, catching my mother in the side of her knee. Her legs came out from under her.

By the time we reached our condominium, she was in considerable pain. A bruise in the shape of a perfect horseshoe had appeared. She had been hospitalized for blood clots in the past. And this time proved no different.

Easily, I could rank this trip in the spot of worst family vacation ever. Actually, I wish I could. Unfortunately, we had others that were worse, just in different ways. To this day, I don't enjoy vacations. I'm more of what you call a stay-cation kind of gal.

So after all was said and done, what lessons could I possibly glean from such an episode? As much as I had been terrified, the horse had protected me in the process of protecting himself. He didn't try to run underneath any of the plentiful tree limbs in an effort to unseat me. He also never reared back in an effort to dump me on the ground.

This protective behavior he displayed was merely a repetition of another time. There was another time in our history, a previous incarnation, when he had felt the need to protect me. Just as every soul I've met has crossed paths with me before, our paths had crossed before.

I had lived in the mountains of North Carolina in the early 1800s. A wood shack had been my family home where I had grown up, learning the "old ways" from my mother and my grandmother. I grew herbs and food in my garden for healing my family and friends. Eventually, I knew so much about the magic of herbs that word spread outside of the community. A spiritual woman, neighbors sought out my help. And because of this, I never left my mountain. But what was worse, I never wanted to. I had learned that leaving the safety of my mountain could only lead to trouble. This was a time when society still feared women with herbal knowledge, *witches*. There still existed taboo against women who could heal. Women like I had been then were often suspected of conspiring with the devil to perform healing miracles.

One day, a man came to my mountain to meet and talk to me. He wanted to write down everything I could teach him into a book. He was a writer, a reporter, who had heard of me and my family. He was a young, eager man. When he arrived, he was overwhelmed by our collective knowledge of the old ways and was excited to document it all.

I trusted him. And in order to protect me from prejudice, this young man kept my identity and the location of my home a secret. And I taught him so much that he felt indebted to me because he became successful in publishing his work.

Fast forward a century and you find this man living a new life as a horse, a spiritual creature, in those same North Carolina mountains. He wanted to return quickly to this place where he had learned so much. But his days are routine, monotonous even, until one day, a young woman arrives. His soul recognizes her instantly even though she does not recognize his. In their previous incarnation, he had learned so much from her about the eternal soul that he learned never to fear death from that time on. Unfortunately, he senses that she has forgotten all that she knew then. Her current religious upbringing, with its absolute rules and black and white dogma, did not leave any room for the individual growth of the human soul. She needed him this time. She could learn from him this time. He would finally get his chance to teach her about spirituality.

He also senses that she doesn't have a lot of experience with riding. As soon as she mounts, he can tell that right away. He also knows that he must be careful with her. Once on the trail, when he senses the yellow jackets' nest, he ran as fast as he could away from it, protecting himself and her from any stings.

Through this episode, even though the results would not come to fruition for decades, I was able to take another step closer to the realization of my past, my spiritual self, and my connection with animals. And through this, my soul took another step forward. I learned that there were and are powers at work that I could not see, did not understand, but were there to protect me. I learned to appreciate the protection Spirit provides to each and every one of us, especially those who experience life-threatening events before their time.

Both of our souls took another step forward that day. We were able to meet again for the distinct purpose of returning a favor. Even though our time was limited, I will never forget that horse. He came into my life at a time when I needed him. And that is how it is with our souls. We return to one another even if for a very brief time. We can rest assured that every one of our experiences is rich with purpose, rich with growth, and rich with history.

Tina Proffitt

5.
George's Story

Come Back

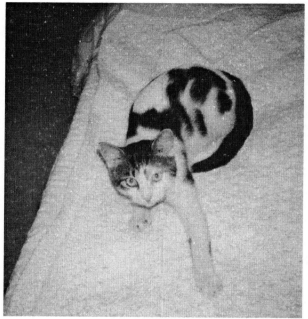

George

When No One Else Did

Still in Texas, I was sixteen; the year was 1991. My parents had enrolled me and my sister in a very large public high school by then, an extreme culture shock I still haven't gotten over. Our private school had been small, only about fifty high school students total. My freshman class alone at this new school contained over nine hundred students. My sophomore English teacher assigned our class a research paper. We were to research the life of a famous writer. And she obligingly supplied us with a list of names. Not surprising to me now over twenty-five years later, the name, Jack Kerouac, jumped out at me.

I didn't know then who he was, but I picked him.

I remember the day I checked out his name in the library, finding him to be a beat poet who wrote books in stream of consciousness. Sitting down at one of the tables in the library that day, I didn't know my life was about to change. I read the first few pages of On the Road. Right then and there, I decided that if anyone could actually get paid to do something as cool as that, then sign me up. Like a bolt of lightning from the sky, I'd just found exactly what I wanted to do with the rest of my life. I walked out of that library a changed young woman. I felt deep inside every fiber of my being, I had discovered my purpose. I didn't know how, or where, or even when. But I would be a *writer*.

My dream did come true, only twenty years later after my thirty-fifth birthday. By this time, I had begun to have vivid dreams at night that I had forgotten my baby, finding him or her in the oddest places like my closet or hamper with the dirty laundry. I remember waking, feeling tremendous guilt over these dreams even though my children were right next to me in the bed. *Were my dreams trying to tell me that I wasn't a good mother?* I feared.

Fortunately, my desire to understand overcame my fear, and I found a book to explore dream meanings, something that according to my upbringing was taboo. I discovered in the dictionaries that dreams are made up of symbols that are metaphors for us to apply to our lives. Most importantly, they are messages from Spirit. My dream was a message from God that I had a forgotten talent or skill waiting to be rediscovered. I needed to pick up where my fifteen-year-old self had left off and start writing. With encouragement from my dear husband, I began writing all the stories I had swimming around in my head on a secondhand laptop we purchased for fifty dollars for just that purpose. And I haven't looked back since, although I do have a new laptop now.

I explore my past in the books I write, drawing on my emotional experiences, changing the circumstances, because I believe in the power of story to heal. In doing this, I experience catharsis. As Meister Eckhart, German monk and mystic, wrote, "To get into the core of God at his greatest, one must first get into the core of himself at his least, for no one can know God who has not first known himself."

My family and I, except my brother, moved back to South Carolina. This time, I was seventeen years old. I left behind my beloved 1981 red, four-door Honda, my room, my friends, my sense of who I was, even my long hair. Every new day I lived the waking nightmare of walking through the metal doors of another public high school, crammed with strangers, full of loneliness and isolation. I trudged through my Senior year, the new girl, not eating, not making eye contact, trying in vain to cut off the pain that radiated from my chest.

I'll never forget, my mother gave me a magnet for my locker. It was the only decoration I allowed it. I purposefully hid myself from these unwanted fellow wanderers. It said, "All things work together for good." I wanted so desperately to believe it. I looked at it every day with the knots wound so tightly in my stomach. I couldn't see it yet, but the verse would one day show itself to be true.

Tina Proffitt

After settling into a rental house near our new high school, my mother took my sister and I to the humane society to adopt a cat. In those days, it was an old house near a small airport in Greenville.

We passed right by the room full of kittens. Everyone wants one of those, we knew. My sister and I were on a rescue mission. There was an adult cat there who needed a home, and we were determined to find them.

George was an adult short-hair with long white whiskers. He popped up as we stepped into the sunny room. The wall of cages lined up against the wall, and while most of the older cats were asleep or indifferent to our arrival, George let us know right away how happy he was to see us. I'd never met a cat I wanted to hold and love more, hence his name. *I will love him and feed him and keep him*—if you watched Looney Tunes as a kid, you know the rest. So his name became George. He was so happy to see us that he rubbed against the cage when we stepped closer. It was definitely one of those love at first sight moments you hear about. You know, your animal picks you, not the other way around.

This was George. He was white with black spots like a Holstein cow, had a round middle, and bright, green eyes. And as soon as he saw us, he began kneading his paws on the floor of his cage as if to say, *I've been waiting for you.*

I couldn't wait to get my hands on him. It *was* love at first sight. And it was love. There's no mistaking it when a relationship is just right.

He preferred to sleep on the foot of my bed where I kept a white afghan (pictured) that my grandmother had

Come Back

knitted for me so my feet wouldn't get cold at night. Every afternoon I came home from school after enduring another day of being the new girl, the new Senior no less in a public high school full of strangers, he was there, waiting for me. I would find him asleep, curled up on the blanket. And as soon as I came in, he would wake up and greet me. He wanted to be there for me because somehow that I didn't comprehend at the time, he knew I needed him.

He had the softest fur, like angora. And he made me feel wanted in a world where I felt anything but. He would stay right there with me as I did my homework after school, listening to music, usually Pearl Jam or The Cure, letting my heart ache. His healing presence was a balm to my wounded soul just as being adopted by a family was to his.

Years later when we moved out of the city and into the county, George would enjoy living on all six acres of land. He roamed, chased mice, enjoyed his freedom, and continued to make me feel loved. There wasn't a day that went by that he didn't greet me at my car when I returned home from school (college by then) then follow me inside. He was the first cat my future husband would say that he ever liked. And for a Proffitt, that's saying a lot.

But George's story, like all souls, was more complicated. His life's purpose was more than just as a house cat or a mouser. His purpose in finding us at the humane society that day was to accomplish another goal. He and I had shared an unrequited love in our past.

It was early 1900s in deep South Carolina where cattle ranches still exist today. We were neighbors. We had grown up together. As we grew, my love for

George's soul grew. I loved George deeply then. But he hadn't shared my feelings. He had been in love with another young woman, my sister. (You see now, as do I, why he chose us both at the same time in the humane society that day.) He had often been in her company and vice versa. The two of them, my sister and George's soul, were the same age, so it was assumed that they were a better match as I was too young for him. (To this day, my younger sister insists she's older than me. You see how the soul remembers?) And although I believed he held feelings for me because of the way I saw him looking at me when we were out with the cows, the two of them eventually married. I had felt betrayed and abandoned because I truly believed that he had loved *me*.

And he, a cat in this life, and, I believe the more consciously aware of the need, was there to make things right between us for his sake as well as mine. The hurt that had at one time been between our souls dissolved in all directions of time when we met again, this time, me as a woman and him as my beloved cat and only friend. George made me feel wanted in a time when the world had rejected me. He made me feel special when the world had shown me otherwise. George was there to let me know that I *was* without a doubt worthy of love. He loved me *with wisdom*.

And because he returned as a cat, he was able to heal this old pain between us in a very few years compared with living another human life. And that, I believe, is the reason souls choose to reappear on Earth as animals. Of course, there are exceptions to this short-lived life, like primates and parrots who live for decades. But our animal companions come into our life, sometimes by surprise, burst in, break our hearts wide open, then leave. And we can feel abandoned by this. But if we can see, if we can feel the underlying purpose that is there inside every one of our relationships with these wise, furry creatures, it is possible to heal past hurts. And with a greater sense of purpose, we can move forward into our future relationships with a sense of what's next?

What's in store for me this time?

What will be healed?

And this can all be done with a sense of looking ahead while at the same time being aware that in looking back we heal our future.

Tina Proffitt

6.
Harley's Story

Come Back

me and Harley

My Hero

It was 1993, the year I graduated from high school. My family had moved onto six wooded acres in Greenville, South Carolina. My boyfriend's mother had offered me a part-time job working at the Baptist church daycare she directed. That way, I could attend morning classes at the local community college. I had been accepted to the University of South Carolina and Clemson where I'd applied, but fear kept me from moving into a dorm with peers. This particular morning, I found myself alone in my parent's house. I didn't have a class. So, I decided I should return the VHS copy of

Tina Proffitt

An Affair to Remember I'd rented to the local video store (back when there were such things) as to avoid a late charge. I collected my Liz Claiborne purse and was on my way out the door when my mother's Doberman Pinscher, Harley, followed me.

It's important to note that up to this point in my relationship with Harley, we had had an understanding. I was afraid of him, and he understood it.

He had come to us, a young man, from a couple who couldn't keep him any longer. His coat was dark red, his ears clipped, his tail docked, and he stood to my waist. He was also a luncheon meat thief. Any unattended sandwiches within Harley's reach would be found by their owners sans meat, bread undisturbed. He also had fixed ideas on where he slept, the couch, even if someone else was on it. And he was, shall we say, intimidating compared with our previous dog, a seventy-five pound English Bulldog, Dolly, whose most aggressive behavior was her habit of passing gas in the car while the windows were rolled up. But intimidating had been exactly what my mother had had in mind when she chose Harley. We were having a little trouble with the previous owner of the house we'd just moved into. The man had been serving time for drug dealing out of the house and for the attempted murder of his ex-partner. He was out, and he wanted his house back. The sheriff's department had been notified of the drug paraphernalia found in one of the barns. A brand new alarm system had been installed. And Harley, intended as a deterrent, moved in.

He did his job well. Ask any of the delivery truck drivers he laid in wait for, biding his time around the corner of the house until they shut off their truck's engine and walked to the door.

This particular day, keys in hand, I stared down at Harley. Nose pointed at the door, he had every intention of coming with me.

Who was this dog? I thought.

Clearly it wasn't Harley. He'd kept his distance from me so much up to this point that I honestly believed he had just mistaken me for someone else. But I was wrong. He wanted to go with me. What I didn't grasp at the time was that Harley was there to do a job—protect our family. And that's exactly what he intended to do.

"I'm going to the video store, Harley," I said, sure he wouldn't want to go. He watched me, still pointed at the door. "I'll be back in a little while." Our house was a good fifteen minutes from town.

He didn't budge.

"Okay," I said, shrugging. And I opened the door.

He led the way to my car parked beneath some trees at the back of the house and waited for me to open the door, the passenger side no less. Then he hopped into the back seat as if we'd done this sort of thing a million times before.

I'm sure my mouth must have hung open the entire drive to town. I couldn't believe what I saw in the rear view mirror. Harley was the perfect passenger. He sat neatly in the back seat, never barking, never even moving. He just watched, observing all the activity around him like any good bodyguard, the kind with earpieces and sunglasses.

Errand completed, we returned home. My parents' house is situated at the back of about six acres. So the driveway cuts across half of it with a clear view of the house from the road. As I approached, there was no car, but I spotted a stranger, a man, standing in front of the house. Harley did too.

But for anyone who knows or has met a Doberman Pinscher, you know that they are not given to hysterics like other dogs sometimes are. Harley saw the man just as clearly as I did, but he didn't begin to bark or scratch at the window to be let out. He waited patiently while I parked at the back of the house, let him out, and secured his leash. Then he let this guy have it!

And I don't mean a warning bark—*Hey! you're not supposed to be here*. He gave him a, I hope you brought a spare set of pants with you, lunging kind of attack bark, the kind you see on TV. I had to brace myself against a tree just to keep from being dragged along behind him.

I tell this story in a fictionalized version in my first romance novel, *Second Chances*, where Harley features as one of the characters, dog, of course. So, it's here that I will pause because it's important to note a few more things about Barney (he's the man standing in my driveway). One, he was a man with a lot of life experience. He was not afraid of Doberman Pinschers because he had raised them for the same purpose Harley had been adopted—to scare people from the property. Two, he wore a camera around his neck, a ruse he'd used before, pretending to be a property investor interested in the house.

He asked me, actually shouted over the barking, if he could take a few pictures of the house. I said yes and turned to go inside. Instead of taking any pictures however, he left.

At this point, a few things ran through my mind. I

knew who this guy was; I wasn't fooled. He'd pulled this real estate investor gambit once before to get back into his former house. The police speculated there was something inside that he'd left behind and wanted back.

Once inside, I called the sheriff's department right away, asking to speak to the sergeant assigned to our case. Barney already had a restraining order against him to keep him away from our house.

I had to leave for work, so a sheriff's deputy arrived a few hours later at the daycare to speak to me, to take my statement.

"He was there when I got home," I said to the officer. "I knew who he was."

"What did you do?"

"I went inside and called Sergeant Williams," I said, thinking that should have been obvious.

"What you should have done," the officer growled, "was call 911!"

I was taken aback. *What did he mean, call 911? It hadn't been an emergency. Nothing had happened!*

Later that night as I prepared for bed and thought about what had happened, I rationalized my behavior. I was a rule follower. I had done the right thing. I had reported the incident to the police. Barney was a dangerous criminal who'd spent time in prison, I knew that. He also was willing to defy a restraining order to get back whatever it was he wanted, I knew that. But that was all, wasn't it? So why had the sheriff's deputy nearly taken my head off? Because try as I might to convince myself that nothing had happened, something very well could have happened. And something indeed had happened—Harley had saved my life.

This man was one bad dude. So, I had no doubt

that that afternoon, Harley had known that he had needed to come with me. He had known that I would need him. He had known that his moment had arrived.

Harley never asked to go for a ride in my car with me again after that day—he didn't need to. He'd done his job, and he'd done it well.

Heaven has given me many chances to learn and grow. Like a loving parent, no one expects a toddler to become an expert at walking on their first solo, it is the same with Heaven. I'm given as long as it takes until I've mastered my lessons.

Whenever I ask to know more about any soul, with their consent, I always ask to consult both their angels and mine.

In Harley's case, he'd come to us, adopted from another family, an orphan. But I discovered that he'd lived a previous incarnation as an orphan. In it, he had become good at taking care of himself. But he had found it difficult to bond with others.

Harley and I had been brother and sister in this previous life, living in a children's home in South Carolina. The doctor who visited the home occasionally to attend to the children was a pedophile. But this was in the early 1950s and that term wasn't common knowledge. One afternoon, the doctor took advantage of an opportunity. He shoved me into a broom closet and molested me. My brother (Harley's soul) had been powerless to stop it. Both of us had been so traumatized by the event that our souls needed to return to meet once again. This time however, Harley was perfectly prepared to defend me and had no trouble in doing so. Because although in this life Barney had been smug, standing his ground instead of running away from the ferocious barking, Harley had prevented him from harming me. Harley was able to fulfill his purpose.

As a Doberman Pinscher, Harley had a lot in the way of survival skills. Can you imagine a fearful or timid Doberman Pinscher? And because of his sureness of self, he *told* me he was coming with me that day, he did not ask. And because of that, I was safe. Because while Barney may not have been frightened of Harley, he had at least a healthy respect for what his teeth could do to him.

So it was through this repetition of becoming an orphan, needing to rely on himself (as much as a domesticated dog can), and through protecting his adopted family, Harley was able to heal.

I was able to see Harley through different eyes from that day forward. He and I had bonded. Even though he continued to keep to himself after that day, I never forgot what he did for me, for both of us. His action and my consent to let him go for a ride had healed us both.

After I married my best friend, Scott, we lived in a new double-wide on an acre at the edge of my parent's property. Shortly after we married, we adopted a sixteen-week-old Labrador puppy, Brittney. Harley and Brittney became the *best* of friends. The two of them were inseparable. One of their favorite pastimes was a tag team effort of flushing out ground squirrels. So Harley became a part of *my* family. Now, he is a piece of my family history, a part of funny stories my husband and I tell our children. He healed that orphaned part of his life in just the few short years he was with us.

Harley died one day years later of a heart condition. His death was sudden. My husband buried him in between our house and my parents' house.

Even though our time with Harley was short, his life was a profound lesson for his soul. He became a part of a family who loved him. He opened his heart to an adorable puppy and showed her how to hunt and how to protect her family. He bonded with us all.

So I will never forget you, Harley.

You're my hero.

Come Back

7.
Brittney's Story

Tina Proffitt

Brittney

Unrequited Love

By the summer of 1995, I'd poured over one too many L.L. Bean catalogues full of pictures of the ideal couple and their charming white Labrador Retriever by their sides. Scott and I were newlyweds, just starting out together. We had moved from his old Spring Creek apartment into a new doublewide so that we could save money. My idea of a perfect family had congealed in my mind, and I figured the best way to start would be with one of those adorable puppies of our own.

Brittney in a lot of ways did become like a child to me. I had had two cats up to this point, but she was the first dog (I could remember) to be mine. Scott and I postponed having children for the first five years of our marriage. During that time, we saved money for a down payment on our house that twenty years later, we still live in, I completed my degree in education at the University of South Carolina, then I taught fifth grade for two years.

Come Back

I missed Brittney so much when I was at work, I used to call from school after my students had gone for the day just to say hello to her over the answering machine or to let her know when I was coming home.

Oftentimes, the house would have been empty had it not been for Brittney. My husband is a career firefighter. His work schedule is twenty-four hours on and forty-eight hours off, which seems like a lot until you factor in his part-time occupation that keeps him away from home during those off forty-eight hours. Brittney slept beside me through every lonely night. She snuggled beside me when I laughed and especially when I cried. She was a constant comfort to me.

Unlike most Labradors, Brittney was afraid of baths, lakes, streams, and even puddles. And I included a true anecdote of her harrowing experience on a hike in my romance novel, *First Forever*.

She was born in North Carolina where she and her siblings were bred to be hunting dogs. Scott and I laid out our two hundred fifty dollars for her, money that Scott had set aside for a new pair of work boots but found he had enough for both. I'll never forget the shock in the breeder's voice when we said we planned to let her live inside the house. "You're going to raise her indoors?"

His wife kind of nudged him in his ribs to stop his protest. I think she recognized the hungry "mother" look in my eyes. Brittney would become my baby, and babies didn't live in the backyard.

We brought her home on a cloud of euphoria. Her coat was the color of cream, just like I'd seen in the magazines. Even as a rambunctious puppy, she was an excellent study for the photographer as my scrap books bear out. She could never leave your tennis shoes tied. I remember the day she discovered that if she held the end of a toilet paper roll in her mouth, it would stream off the roll behind her like a banner as she ran from the bathroom. She could do no wrong. She was all mine. And she was always there for me. In a very real way, she was the first animal (I could remember) to teach me about unconditional love.

Naming Brittney would become my only dilemma. I knew I wanted to name her Brittney, but as I'd learned there were two ways to spell it. Brittney and Brittany. I wanted to name her Brittany, it just felt right. But my best friend in Texas had an older sister with the same name. And because I was starting a new life here in South Carolina, I didn't want to choose that name even though I preferred it. (I would find out later why.) So, I chose the name Brittney. Although I did not name her after her, there was a delightful little girl whom I cared for at the day care with the same name. So the association with this spelling was more in keeping with my new life since the day care is where I met my husband.

One of my most common refrains to Brittney as the two of us sat on the floor of the living room watching television was, "I wish you could talk". My favorite show at the time was about a British medium, who would talk to people's animals who had passed over. Little did I know at the time that Brittney *could* talk—and she did. I just needed to learn to *hear* in a different way than I was used to.

Brittney's body has been gone now for six and a half years, and the loss sometimes still feels fresh. But I know that she is not truly gone. In the words of Obi-

Come Back

Wan Kenobi, "If you strike me down, I shall become more powerful than you can possibly imagine." And so it is with Brittney. When her body finally quit, she became a powerful, eternal force of energy in my life that I can never be without. She is my constant companion when I communicate in the spiritual etheric plane.

She especially loved being in the woods surrounding my parent's home. That is where she and Harley did their work of hunting and patrolling. One of my favorite snap shots is of her (pictured), lying on the cool ground beneath those trees, leaves resting all around her, a contented smile on her face.

One of her previous lives had been as a member of my family in the woods of North Carolina where we were healers. She, my son in that incarnation, took great comfort being among the trees. In that life, our family was by today's standards very poor. We grew our own food and herbs for medicine. We had little money, and what little we had was shared among the family including extended family. Because of this, Brittney's soul felt the need to leave. She felt that there was not enough to provide for her needs, so she traveled, seeking her own fortune.

Leaving home had been very difficult for her soul. Because she was forced to wander, she dearly missed being a part of a family. Her soul longed to return to me, her mother in that incarnation, and to be a part of a family once more. When her soul finally did return though, my soul had passed over.

This time, when her soul returned as our dog, she was able to meet that need to be a family again. Because my husband and I had no children when she came to us and for the first five years of her life, she was able to be the center of my world. That part of her that had felt there wasn't enough resources to go around was able to heal.

In yet another incarnation, Brittney and I had lived before, she had not returned my feelings of love for her. She, being a woman in that incarnation and me a man, had been in love with another man. So she returned to me in this life to be my devoted best friend, a constant companion who never left my side, for fifteen long but too short years, thereby healing that hurt for the both of us.

So in her life as a dog, she was able to heal two past lives with me. But her lessons were not only with me, but also with Harley.

Harley as I said earlier, was older than she by many years. He, a dominant Doberman Pinscher was used to barking orders. But instead of being an abusive authority figure, he guided Brittney, leading by example instead of force. The two of them together were a sight to behold. She, at sixteen weeks old, meeting Harley for the first time, and he, standing over her like a gentle giant, were a match made in Heaven. They missed each other. They spent every day together. They were soulmates.

During that previous life in the North Carolina mountains, living deep in the woods, Harley's soul had also been there. His soul had been in a woman's body, a midwife. She had been there when Brittney's soul was born into our family. Harley's soul in that life had longed for her own children but was unable to have any of her own. Her calling was to help bring other women's babies into the world. Because of this, she felt a deep connection to each and every baby she helped enter the world. Her relationship with Brittney's soul was no different. And when Brittney's soul grew up and left the mountain, she felt the loss deeply.

When Brittney and Harley were reunited, the soul connection was instantaneous, a unification of two souls who had loved before. So theirs' was a reunion of souls coming together out of love, to heal.

That is the way it is with all souls. Whatever it is in our past can be healed.

I loved Brittney with all my heart, still do.

And the best part is, so does she.

Tina Proffitt

8.
Todd's Story

Come Back

Todd

Letting Go

Todd came to live with us about a year and a half after Scott and I were married. Brittney was full-grown by that time. I was in school full-time, driving forty-five minutes one way to attend classes at the University of South Carolina's Spartanburg campus. I spent most of my days there, studying, then eventually doing practicums. Scott was gone much of the time as well. He was on duty for twenty-four hours at a time then left straight from his fire station to arrive at his part-time job without coming home in between. So I worried about the amount of time Brittney spent alone. I felt that if only we could get another dog, she wouldn't be lonely while we were away.

One day, my husband, Scott, phoned me from his station. He said there was a Jack Russell Terrier there that had just appeared out of the blue. Thinking that it had gotten free from its fencing, he had put the terrier back into one of the neighboring yards where he felt sure he had come from. A few hours later though, the Jack Russell had reappeared in the backyard of the fire station. And according to the homeowners surrounding the station, he didn't belong there. Now they had a problem, because the station faced one of the busiest roads in Greenville, Pelham Road. After speaking with some of the other shifts, Scott discovered that they too had seen this little fellow. And no, no one knew where he had come from.

I, of course, upon learning about this poor dog's plight, had gotten so excited that I insisted he bring the dog home with him the next day.

As I looked into the adorable dog's eyes for the first time, I knew it wasn't love at first sight, but it was definitely exciting. Todd was good-looking and smart. I felt that surely my prayers for a friend for Brittney had been answered. We took him to the vet right away. His shots up to date, we made an appointment for him to be neutered in about two weeks. This would give us time to find his owner. In the meantime, we ran an ad in the newspaper for a found dog. We received many, many hopeful calls, but alas, none of them for him.

The good news for me was that Brittney seemed semi-interested in this spirited newcomer. Scott fenced in the backyard so that the two of them would have a safe place to be outside.

They made a daily ritual of playing together in the

Come Back

living room, rolling and nipping as dogs will do. This went on for some time until Brittney had finally had enough. But Todd (named for the band, Big Head Todd and the Monsters) would not hear of stopping. He continued to bark at her, to bite her ears. She stoically ignored him. And he eagerly pursued her. This became their daily ritual. She ignored him, and he annoyed her.

Todd never sat still. He would spend hours on end outside, springing off the ground in an attempt to catch carpenter bees. He did the same thing in the kitchen when he found Scott eating a banana.

Meanwhile, I tried to connect with Todd in some way, in any way. I wanted so badly to love him. But when I looked into his eyes, all I got was a shifty stare that told me he had other places to be.

The afternoon we brought him home from the vet clinic from being neutered, I gingerly placed him in his bed, carefully making sure that he had everything he needed. To my utter dismay, he growled at me.

My heart hurt. This was more than a simple reaction to a dog expressing his pain. His growl was a deeply felt rejection. What I didn't realize at the time was that he and I were simply replaying a scene that had played out centuries before. Todd and I had a connection that went beyond our brief acquaintance in this life. He had betrayed me in love in a previous incarnation. In ancient Ireland, I had been a healer, living among the forest. I had knowledge of herbal medicines. He had come to me injured, badly in need of care. I had healed him. I had loved him. And he had callously tossed me aside, leaving me after he had healed.

Ultimately, in Todd's relentless pursuit of other

things like bananas and bees and unsuccessful attempts to play with Brittney, we did not bond, he and I. He and Brittney had not bonded. In fact, instead of becoming a friend to Brittney, he became a problem. Brittney became withdrawn. She was unable to take naps without being pounced on. She couldn't sit up without having her ears nipped. There was no peace for her in our house. Todd needed a different family. But I just couldn't send him packing, not yet.

Then one night, the decision to find another home for Todd was made for us. My husband and I had gone out to dinner, leaving Todd in his crate. Arriving home after dark, we stepped into the house to find an odd pile of paper on the floor.

Brittney and Todd stood over the pile. (Don't ask me how Todd got out of his crate, because I don't know.) At first our minds did not register what we saw. Then slowly but surely the pieces fell into place. The two dogs stood in front of the bookshelf Scott and I had built by hand. One large tome, a beloved heirloom given to Scott by his now late father, was absent from the bookshelf.

Brittney had never chewed up a book or even piece of paper in her life. Her teething days were long behind her. So we knew instantly who the instigator of this catastrophe was.

Our copy of <u>The Story of Civilization</u> by Will Durant from 1957, had been a hardback so large that the two of them must have spent the entire two hours we had been out of the house working on it. It was completely unrecognizable as having ever been a book, if not for the tiny shreds of green cardboard that had only hours before been its cover.

Come Back

I felt guilty. I felt horrible. Todd was not happy and was letting us know. Now Todd would be out a home, and Brittney would be out a friend. But it was decided we would try to do what was best for him. In the animal supply store the following day we saw a business card beside the register—a woman who bred Jack Russell Terriers. It was like a beacon of light from Heaven. We asked the woman behind the counter if she knew her, and she said she did. We told her that we had a purebred Jack Russell, but he had already been neutered so would be of no use for breeding. We asked her if she thought that this woman would still be interested. She said that the woman had recently lost one of her own Jack Russells who had been hit by a car and would most certainly be interested in meeting him.

We called her and discovered that she had ten acres of treed land and four other Jack Russells that had the run of the place. Ours was only a quarter of an acre of fenced backyard and a disinterested Labrador. It was agreed that she would drive to our house to pick up Todd as soon as possible. I felt happy for Todd and relieved that he would be going to what sounded like Jack Russell Heaven.

When the day arrived, miraculously, upon meeting this woman, this hyperactive, near obsessive dog became a bundle of goo. She scooped him up and held him like a baby in her arms, never letting him go as they gazed into each other's eyes. It was definitely love at first sight.

Before she left with him, she insisted that she pay us. But we insisted even more that all we wanted was for him to be happy.

Looking back on this episode with Todd, I can only

feel grateful that the two of them found each other as they were surely meant to. Scott, Brittney, and I had merely been a temporary family for Todd.

By our paths crossing however briefly again in this life, I was able to assist him once again as I had in Ireland. I was able to show him the forgiveness for abandoning me that his soul longed for. This was the reason he and I had come together again. The hurt that he had caused me so long ago was erased. With compassion towards him, I helped him find his way to his happiness. In doing so, we were able to heal our previous relationship.

Because of Todd's previous incarnation in Ancient Irish culture, he believed in the power of plants to heal. He lived among the trees, spoke to them. Some Jack Russells are even known to climb trees. In this life, Todd's soul needed to return to nature in order to progress. Confinement by fences and the confusion of busy cities were all too much for him. Some can only hear Spirit's messages in the peace and tranquility of the woods. I can relate.

And at our home, things with Brittney improved on their own without any help from another dog. My husband and I had simply been a rest stop for Todd on his journey, a place for him to wait for another family to come and pick him up. But that's okay. Sometimes, we are just that for each other. We help each other through transitions. Instead of Todd being homeless for who knows how long, he was provided a warm place to sleep and food to eat from people who wanted to love him.

And even though ours was not a love match, I will never forget Todd. He will always have a place in my heart and a place in my scrapbook.

Letting him go was not an easy decision, but when I listened to my heart, I knew the answer. For Todd's sake, for his happiness, I needed to.

Todd's journey from the fire station to our home had been a small part of his spirit's journey. We were never actually meant to become his permanent family.

We were just meant to help him find his.

Tina Proffitt

9.
Kitty's Story

Come Back

Kitty

I Love You to Death

Kitty burst into our lives quite suddenly.

One afternoon as my son rode his Big Wheel and my daughter and I drew pictures in sidewalk chalk on our driveway, a loud, persistent meowing began, like a fire truck's siren, something as kids of a firefighter they were very familiar with. The cry was so loud in fact that my son screeched to a halt on his trike and my daughter flew into my arms. I scooped her up and the three of us, huddled together, became very still, waiting for this beautiful gray, short hair to make it up the drive. I knew the best way to scare away a cat is to make sudden moves, so I held my breath. I didn't want to take any chances.

A family of stray cats live right on the outskirts of our neighborhood. *But certainly one of those cats would never approach humans*, I thought. This cat cried out for our help. It didn't take a psychic to know that.

After some discussion as to what we would do, the three of us went inside to get some cat food. Only I didn't have any cat food. I didn't even have a small enough bowl. We lived with a Labrador Retriever who ate out of bowl bigger than this cat. I scrounged around the pantry and found a can of tuna. *No*, I thought. *If I give her straight tuna and she's starved, she might get sick. She needs some carbs too.* Why I reasoned all this, I don't know. So I found a can of sweet peas and mixed them into the tuna. I served this mixture on a paper plate on our front porch. We watched amazed as she devoured every bite. I've never seen a cat eat so voraciously. And it was obvious from the way her belly sagged, she was a new mother. My heart broke for her.

I had wanted to adopt a cat for many years. I missed George. But I didn't see the point in adopting a cat before our children were born due to the inevitable litter box issues during pregnancy. I had at one time wanted four children. But after my daughter was born, my husband and I looked at each other and decided two children was enough, one for each of us, in the spirit of teamwork. So this cat appearing out of nowhere had to be Heaven-sent.

I told my children that if we wanted to keep her, we could make a bed for her on the porch and give her a water bowl. But we would need to take her to the vet for a check-up. Moments later, my husband got the call at work that he has since learned to dread—*Would it be okay with you if we keep her?*

"Did you find the right family?" the vet asked her the next day after he confirmed that she was indeed healthy. "But," he then said to us, "if she's already lived most of her probably two years on Earth outdoors, she may never become a house cat."

That was okay. I welcomed the chance. Plus, we'd already fallen in love.

Kitty officially became her name. My kids, four and seven at the time, named her. We had her spayed. And she became an official member of the Proffitt family, the first of her kind. The Proffitt's side of the family are *not* known as cat-lovers.

It was confirmed by the vet that she had already had a litter of kittens. This led to countless questions from my children: *Where are the kittens now? Why didn't they stay together? If she's their mommy, doesn't she miss them?*

And to be honest, these were questions that I had too. Had someone simply dropped her off in our neighborhood, counting on some generous soul to care for her? I suspected as much.

"Animals are different than humans," I said to my children.

That's the simple answer. The more complicated ones were yet to come.

For about the next six months, Kitty enjoyed living inside. She bonded with Brittney, even shared her bed. My children were happy to have a little animal to pick up and hold. And she didn't seem to mind all the attention in the slightest. Apparently the vet had been wrong. So it came as quite a surprise to me when she one day bolted out an open door and abjectly refused to come back when called. My heart broke. *She doesn't love me as much as I love her*, I thought. I felt rejected by this gray beauty to whom I had given my heart.

But the next day, there she was, asking to come back inside. Joy reigned again. Then a few days later, she left again. This went on for some time. And the time in between her return visits became longer.

One day after several days in a row of not seeing Kitty, I asked my next door neighbor if she had seen her. The neighbor who lived two houses down from ours happened to overhear and later reported that he and his wife fed a cat that they had named Smokey, a gray, short hair who some nights slept in their garage with their cat. I was shocked. Kitty had more than one family?

As more time passed, we heard from another neighbor that yes, he also fed a gray cat. And then another and another until we discovered the whole street knew our Kitty and thought she was their cat too.

My heart was divided. On one hand, I was happy that Kitty had so many people who loved her. She is one of the most affectionate cats I've ever met. She's one of those cats who's never met a stranger, will walk right up to you. But on the other hand, I felt the need to stake a claim. So, in turn, I gently let each neighbor know that we paid for Kitty's shots and visits to the vet. She was indeed ours. But this roaming was too much.

Then something brought it to a complete and utter stop. One Saturday this past summer, a particularly hot day, I called Kitty from our front porch. I scooped her up. She is a short-legged cat and back then weighed seven pounds on a good day. This day, she was thinner than I thought she should be. Between the heat and her insistence on living outside, she looked so frail. I'd

Come Back

finally had enough.

Since then, Kitty has been moved back inside. I cannot in good conscience allow Kitty to live outdoors *and* tolerate the constant threat of fights with feral cats that encroach upon her territory in ever increasing numbers. She had in many ways belonged to our street. But over the years most of those neighbors have moved away. And she was ultimately my responsibility.

But Kitty's life as a homeless soul was nothing new. In a previous incarnation she had grown up an orphan. Just as she had been dropped off in our neighborhood by her previous owners, she had been without a family to love her in her previous life.

When I learned this, I literally gasped. Now everything made sense. Kitty had returned to relive that lost child part of herself in order to heal it.

We had adopted her. *We* had made her a part of our family. If she knew just one thing about these humans, it was that *we* wanted her. She was an orphan no longer.

Kitty also has another part of her soul, the part that longs to be a part of the outdoors, to commune with nature. I struggle with my need to protect her and the need to allow her her freedom. She is tough. She has taken care of herself in the past. I can't count how many scrapes she came home with during those years she roamed, a bitten ear, a bite on her neck, a hurt paw.

But she is a part of an even larger family now. During those years that Kitty refused to live inside, my children wanted cats of their own. They each adopted a cat from the shelter. And since Kitty has moved back inside now too, there are three cats living inside as siblings who love each other and enjoy occasional bouts of Greco-Roman wrestling.

Tina Proffitt

And here's where our history, Kitty's and mine, comes together. The hardest part of loving Kitty for me has been fighting my urge to protect her from the world completely, to close her up inside the safety of four walls. My heart wants her to be inside the house where I can *know* she is safe. I felt a tremendous amount of anger and guilt on those days when I had to patch up her bites and scratches from the street cats. But her heart tells her to wander. And after all, she is here to live her life, not the one I want for her.

A previous incarnation as a knight, yes, the kind that wore the shining armor, sheds a lot of light on why I feel so protective of my beautiful damsel. She and I have a history together. She was, in a previous incarnation, my daughter. I loved her with my whole heart as any father would. But I lost her to an accident that I could have prevented.

She had wanted to learn to ride a horse more than anything. I told her that she would have to wait, despite her protests that other children learned to ride. I finally relented. I taught her to ride on my horse. One day, the horse spooked. She fell and died from her injuries. Being a knight's daughter then must be, to my mind, like being the daughter of a policeman or fireman today. Police officers and firefighters are keenly aware of the dangers that lurk around every corner. Allowing their children to grow up in a world fraught with perils must be mind-bogglingly difficult. And a loving father of a daughter would not allow his child to step foot near any kind of danger.

I am still learning my lesson with Kitty. For now, she lives inside. She loves spending time on the screened porch. I'm not against her living outside when

Come Back

it becomes safe again. As Kitty's adopted "mother", I feel it is my responsibility to ensure her safety. Ultimately, I have to ask myself, *Would I be able to live with her death as a result of something I could have prevented?*

Nowadays, when the door is opened, she does not try to run out. She is eleven years old and healthy with many years ahead of her. We will work it out before all is said and done. She is learning that being a part of a family means sometimes feeling a little smothered. She is teaching me the importance of loving her philosophically, that is, *to love with wisdom.* Sometimes loving someone means making unpopular choices. In any case, it's good practice for *loving* my teenagers *with wisdom.*

Tina Proffitt

10.
Puss in Boots' Story

Come Back

Puss in Boots

Hungry Heart

Puss in Boots, named after the Shrek cat, also known as, Puss-Puss, is a round orange tabby. Imagine a famous orange cat who graced the funny papers for decades, and you have Puss.

Brittney was getting on in years by now. She couldn't play like she used to. My kids wanted animal friends of their own.

On a trip to the humane society, Puss wasted no time in spotting my son. He meowed, looking like a tiny lion in a cage. He pawed at the cage door, telling my son in no uncertain terms to get him out of there.

According to the vet working there that day, Puss had only been in the cage for about ten or fifteen minutes. This was his first morning. And it was definitely one of those times when the animal picks the person.

My daughter had her eye a beautiful white kitten who was deaf. But living in a neighborhood full of dogs, I didn't know if that was safe. What if the cat got out?

I told her we should sleep on it, and if the cat was still there the next day, we would take her home. Alas, the white cat was adopted by someone else that very day.

Puss became an instant part of our family. He and my son spent hours bonding. After playing, Puss would curl up in my son's lap and fall asleep. They would remain that way until it was time to play again. My son learned vital lessons about loving an animal's soul. He worried about him, fed him, and made sure he was happy and safe.

And it didn't take long to notice that this tiny kitten seemed very hungry, a lot hungrier than Kitty. Every time I went into the laundry room, he followed, meowing for his bowl to be refilled (something he still does to this day). And every time, I was sure that I had just refilled it. But he purred and rubbed against my arms until I gave in. I rationalized that he was very rambunctious and as a result, very hungry.

So, slowly but surely over the space of two years, without us even noticing the change, he turned into a very round adult cat. He now resembled the Shrek IV Puss in Boots. Aside from his being overweight, Puss has a clean bill of health. Yet as overweight as he is, he behaves like he is starved, oftentimes devouring his food so fast that he throws it up minutes later. We tried canned food to provide him a sense of more fullness. Nothing has worked one hundred percent. And *Poor*

Come Back

Puss! has become a popular refrain from me. His life revolves around eating. I could relate.

At first, I projected onto him my own problem with food, that it was his one source of reliable happiness. So I fed him when he asked me to, and at the same time we made a concerted effort to provide more toys and activities for him. He loves to chase shadows and lasers. But even during his outings into the backyard to explore, he ate the various grasses growing out there, then came inside and threw up.

Puss' problem with food I discovered had nothing to do with boredom or unhappiness. He was frightened—afraid that the food in front of him would be his last. Finally, the pieces fell into place. The racing ahead of me to the laundry room, almost tripping me to get to his food bowl to say it's empty, the desperate cries for food after just finishing a bowl, were all a result of his having been deprived of enough food in his previous life.

Puss reincarnated from a life in which he had literally starved to death. He and I had been an extremely poor family. As Puss' father in that life, I could not support us all. We lived in a community of people, who after a terrible drought, during which all of our food supply withered and died, all starved to death. His soul carries the memory of this horrible, slow death. And my soul carried the memory of the tremendous guilt I felt for this.

I unconsciously tried to assuage my guilt by overfeeding Puss now.

My feelings of parental love for him make a lot more sense in this light. Often, I even hear myself slip up and call Puss by the same nickname I use for my son.

Tina Proffitt

The best solution I have come up with so far to his overeating is to feed him small amounts of food at a time several times a day. An egg-shaped cat feeder gives him a fun way to eat slowly and keeps me from tripping over him on one of his former tears into the laundry room to his empty bowl. I eat several small meals throughout the day myself. That way, I know I can always eat again in a little while. And now when I feed Puss, I reassure him that he can have more when he's ready, just as I do myself. I stroke him while he eats and tell him how much I love him. I remind him that there's no danger of him starving in this life.

I can take comfort in knowing that he will not starve to death under my care this time. And he has healed that part of him that is so hungry, hungry to know that he is indeed safe. For he is and will continue to be well-fed—heart, soul, and body.

Come Back

11.
Petey's Story

Petey

911

I woke up this particular morning in April, my husband at the fire department, with a *great* idea, I thought.

Brittney had just lost her appetite. She was fifteen years old, had arthritis in her hip, and couldn't navigate stairs any longer. In hindsight, I can see it wasn't so much of a great idea I'd had as a blind panic.

I needed a puppy to bring Brittney's interest in eating back. And I needed one ASAP! I'd read about things like this working to bring pep back to an old dog's life.

My kids and I loaded into the truck and headed for the humane society. I knew we needed a puppy for this job, so we headed right for their area. With startling clarity, I spotted him from across the room. He was white and had a brown patch over his right eye, right out of The Little Rascals. It was Petey!

The sign on his cage said, Boxer Mix. I scooped his little eight-week-old body out of the cage and sat down to hold him. He must have sensed my urgency. There was no way he couldn't have, but he took it in stride, wagging his tail and nibbling my fingertips. As I sat there, looking at all of his cuteness and feeling stunned by my luck in finding him so quickly, another woman approached.

"Are you going to take him home?" she asked rather expectantly.

My fingers reflexively closed around him as if I were afraid she would take him away. And there was no way I was giving him up. He was Petey. And he had a job to do.

"Yes, I am," I declared. I just had to call my husband first.

We went into the getting-to-know-you room so that we could put him on the floor and interact with him. At this point, I was so elated, I wouldn't have minded if he had bitten me. I was taking him home.

While we played with him, I made my urgent call to Scott. I made thoroughly sure that he was okay with me bringing home a puppy, assuring him that this little guy would make a good fit. He was just so cute, how could he not?

We filled out our paper work, promising to return him to the humane society if we decided not to keep him. *No way that was going to happen*, I thought.

As we all took our places in the truck, Petey really chomped down on one of my fingers. Now, I have been around plenty of puppies in my day, but never had I felt such a powerful bite from an eight-week-old puppy. But in my euphoria, nothing slowed me down.

We drove right to the fire department to show Scott the newest member of our family.

Nothing brings firemen out of a station faster than puppies, well maybe a few other things do, but the puppy did the job. And soon we were surrounded by a crowd of on-lookers, me and Petey. I set him down on the ground so that everyone could have a good look. He had that adorable puppy way of walking sideways! As I looked on, the proud new momma to this bundle of cuteness, I overheard some words that nearly stopped my heart.

"You say that's a boxer mix?" one of the firemen said to my husband. "Don't look like any boxer I ever saw. He's a pit."

As his last words echoed in my mind, my internal dialogue went something like this, "Noooooooo!"

He couldn't be. He wasn't. I wouldn't let him. I didn't know how to handle a dog like that. I preferred sweet, goofy dogs, not intellectually gifted dogs who could strategize. I wouldn't think about it. He had a higher calling here. He had to rescue Brittney!

I wish I could say my cock-eyed plan had worked. It didn't. Brittney knew it was her time. And as much as it hurt me, I had to respect that.

At this point, I rationalized, maybe having Petey with us would soften the blow. It didn't.

For the next two months, Petey grew to almost his full size. He was handsome. He was funny. He would sneak up behind us and give our backsides little nibbles. And, like the fireman had said, he was not a boxer. He was a Staffordshire Terrier. He was also very territorial.

Come Back

Our neighbors behind us have a back yard that backs up to ours. They also have about four or five dogs at all times. One of them, my family and I had recently fallen in love with. He had tunneled under the fence to come visit us. As best as I could tell, and admittedly I am not good at spotting breeds, he is a mix of Dachshund (how fitting) and Corgi. He's adorable and one of the sweetest dogs I've ever met. Five minutes after he came into our yard, my daughter had him cradled in her arms like a baby on his back, and he was loving it!

A few weeks of this passed. I admit, I looked forward to looking out my kitchen window and seeing that Massie had come for another visit. Unfortunately, one afternoon, Petey was in the yard as well. Upon seeing Massie come through the fence, Petey rushed to him. The fight that ensued was over in less than thirty seconds but left both dogs bloodied. Petey stepped away unscathed however—he wore Massie's blood. Scott volunteered to carry Massie home, wounded.

A million things ran through my head. What if our neighbors called the police or sued us? (They didn't. They took it rather amazingly as a matter of fact.)

"Dogs will do that kind of thing," she'd said.

I guess you don't have five dogs living with you without the occasional outburst.

Still, the rational mother side of me said we couldn't keep an aggressive dog in a neighborhood full of family pets and little children. Suddenly, I had nightmarish visions of him chained to a cinder block in some dirt yard. All Petey had known up to that point was laughter and play and love. *No, don't do this to yourself*, I thought. Our county had mercifully just outlawed such animal cruelty. I decided right then and there to hold Petey's future in a positive light in my mind. I would not fear for him. I would imagine the best possible scenario, a loving couple who saw his sweet, fun-loving nature, people who would make him a part of their family, a great future. We had just been his transition family, a foster family, if you will. We had shown him that people can be trusted and loved. I had to believe that. I still do.

We returned him to the humane society as promised, a bag of his food and his collar that said *Petey*. I rubbed his floppy ears, and he wagged his tail. I cried as I said goodbye. He looked into my eyes and licked my fingers as if to say, I love you too.

Ours is a no-kill shelter and the assistant who received Petey said, "This cute little guy won't be here long."

And I hoped he wouldn't. And I hoped that whoever picked him up would love him even more than we had. And what I was about to find out about Petey's previous life was going to bring all of this into crystal clear focus.

Petey's soul's purpose in coming back this time was to learn to express himself—to truly be his authentic self. In the years of the Civil War, from the year 1861 to 1865, he had been the adult son of a powerful woman, a wealthy woman, who'd dominated his life. He was not allowed to express himself, his thoughts or his emotions. He avoided confrontations with her. He refused to stand up to her. And it was because of his domineering mother that he'd left home to become a soldier. Petey's soul had been powerless in his own home growing up, and he decided that he would take his life into his own hands literally. He signed up to become a Confederate soldier and died on the battlefield, a young man afraid of conflict, he had died in a bloody fight to the death.

Petey survived his fight with Massie. In fact, if he were keeping score, he might say he won that battle. He did not fear the confrontation. As a matter of fact, he instigated it.

Petey's soul returned to Earth as what the law defines as a "potentially dangerous" dog, commonly referred to by the nickname for the "pits" they are fought in. But he was not adopted by a family who wanted him to fight. He was adopted by a loving family who wanted him for all the love he had inside him. Nevertheless, Petey expressed himself fully. He was unapologetically himself. He was a dog doing what nature dictated—defending his boundaries because they'd been threatened. But because he wasn't punished for what he'd done nor was he encouraged to do it again, he was able to see that being the dog he came here to be was going to be okay. He could work through his lesson in safety.

I was the one who spotted Petey that day in the humane society. I was the one who wouldn't back down when the woman who wanted him as well approached me, because my soul recognized Petey's soul. I had also known Petey's soul in that previous life. Petey's soul and my soul had wanted to marry, something that his controlling mother had forbidden. And because Petey died young on that battlefield, we had never been able to marry.

In this life, Petey's soul is learning to confront, to use his anger to protect his boundaries. How better to accomplish that than to become the embodiment of a "fighting" dog, to became that which he had feared.

In this second chance, our souls were given the opportunity to heal. Petey and I reunited as loving "mother" and loving animal. He received love from me while expressing his anger, something his previous mother had been unable to do. And I was able to love him through his self-expression, thereby healing his fear of conflict.

Saying goodbye to Petey was heart-wrenching, yet necessary. We had perfectly played our parts for each other. And I know that Petey went on to live a happy life—still is living a happy life somewhere, free to be exactly who he truly is, an animal with a right to express himself.

Maybe the woman who'd wanted him came back for him. Maybe not. But one thing I know for sure, whoever took Petey home was meant to for his soul's sake—just as I had been.

Come Back

12.
Duke's Story

Tina Proffitt

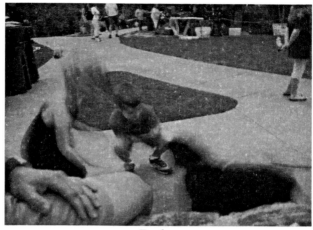

Duke

One Night Stand

Duke was in my life for only one evening, but I will never forget him. A one-night stand is something I've never experienced, but I guess I could draw a parallel because that evening was something I'll never forget.

It was May of 2009. Duke was the first Bernese Mountain Dog I'd ever met. I'd never even heard of the breed before that night, and I, like many others upon hearing the name of the breed for the first time, thought the man had said, Burmese, like the python. But this exquisite dog is called Bernese after the Bern's mountains in Switzerland. They have long, full hair, not fur, with a thick undercoat. And they're beautiful.

Duke was aptly named and a guest like me and my family at the inaugural production of Shakespeare in the

Come Back

Park. My kids and I had recently studied *Romeo and Juliet* and thought this would be a perfect way to kick off our summer break.

Duke's owner sat on the edge of a brick retaining wall, holding the leash of his other dog, a Newfoundland puppy.

My family and I sat behind him on the grassy hill that made up the stadium for the play going on below.

Duke, to my great delight, began making rounds through the crowd, dragging his leash behind him but never straying too far from his human. Duke greeted anyone and everyone who wanted to meet him. I'd never seen anything like it (and as I said before, I grew up in a time before leash laws were enforced). It was like watching a priest bless the members of a crowd one by one. And after what felt like an excruciatingly long wait, he finally made his way over to me. His well-mannered disposition only added to his handsomeness with one blue and one brown eye. The amazing thing about Duke, and I would learn about the breed itself, was that he didn't just greet you—he came as close as you would let him, looking into your eyes. And he didn't pant or drool. He just gazed deep into your soul.

I was entranced. Looking into his eyes felt like staring into the face of pure love. I couldn't get enough. I couldn't get enough of him, the feel of his exquisitely soft hair beneath my hands, the way his face smiled, the way he made me feel as if I were the only person in that park. And then it happened. As he looked into my eyes, I "heard" him say, *healing.*

And that was all he said, but it was as clear a word to my mind as anything I've ever heard a human being utter.

Tina Proffitt

Healing.
I rolled the word around in my mind, watching him drift back into the crowd.

"Wait!" I thought to myself. "Come back! Is there more?"

But there were more fans of his waiting their turn. And although Duke did make his way back around to me once more before the night was over, he said no more. He had given me my message.

I told that story at one of my animal communication classes. Jann Howell, my teacher, said, "That's wonderful that you *heard* the word."

I learned from her that everyone has the ability to communicate with animals. But like any skill, it takes practice. And most people either hear, see, of feel their messages.

Duke was my divine messenger. He and I were there at that Shakespeare play that night for that purpose—communicating. For him, delivering his message was as natural as breathing. For me, an initiate, hearing the message was life-changing. A dog had spoken to me without barking. I would never be the same.

Duke was here on Earth to learn to express his emotions, particularly his love for his fellow creatures. Can you imagine a better way to accomplish that goal than to become one of the most effusive dogs on the planet?

Duke knew I needed to forgive, to heal. Through the infinite divine wisdom that permeates the universe, he knew of my need to forgive my parents. His mission was to instigate change in me. And it worked! His message catapulted me into action.

Come Back

I became a woman on a mission. For the next several weeks, I researched Bernese Mountain Dogs. I learned everything I could about them. I found the closest breeder to us and contacted them.

We had said goodbye to Brittney in May of 2008. This was a year later. We had been a dog family without a dog. And I was finally ready to open my heart to another Earth Angel.

I'd decided I had to have one of those dogs for my very own. Just the memory of Duke wouldn't do. And I would have one if it was the last thing I ever did. And have one, I did. We brought Juliet home from Asheville, North Carolina on November 15, 2009.

Tina Proffitt

13.
Juliet's Story

Come Back

Juliet

Stobs

If you are unfamiliar with the term, stobs, don't worry. I think most people are. It is a Scottish word that refers to boundary markers. Some states, like Alabama for instance, go so far as to define what constitutes a stob. Stone, metal, or plastic are used nowadays as boundary markers on land because they won't blow away or disintegrate quickly. Some stone land markers found in the British Isles date as far back as the early medieval times.

I first heard the word used by my father when my husband and I were marking off the boundary (for tax purposes) between my parents' land and ours.

Since lack of personal boundaries were an issue when I was growing up, Juliet showed up to become my teacher. Since day one she has taught me about boundaries.

Admittedly, I still have trouble with mine. Don't get me wrong—boundaries are good and necessary. I work best within well-defined boundaries.

"You have wet noodle boundaries," my therapist said. And I agreed.

Upon one fall trip to the beach, Juliet greeted most passersby with a wagging tail. I held her leash as she happily let strangers approach and pet her. But there was one man in particular. He patted her head and spoke to her and drifted away. But when he returned for another visit, this time when my husband and children had gone into the surf, she wouldn't have it. She barked, and barked, and barked. Even the man remarked, surprised that she'd let him pet her only minutes before. Looking back on the episode, I can only surmise that Juliet was protecting me from this man. I had been alone. She was establishing a boundary for me that I was unable to establish for myself.

I sometimes wish for nothing less than me and my family living and working together in the same space, like a pre-industrial age village. I've even shared this notion with my children, to the chagrin of my therapist. I can see her shaking her head at me. A true Pisces, I'm as watery as my boundaries, wanting to be close yet maintaining the ability to swim away and hide under a rock at will.

In the process of writing this book, I passed through the hallway one afternoon and found my "baby", Juliet, lying on her side. Her back was against the wall and her feet stretched out in front of her. I leaned over her. Now was my chance, I thought. She never lets me kiss her. If I come at her from overhead,

Come Back

she head-butts me. If I come from the side, she dodges. I knelt in front of her. She had no escape route. I kissed her cheek. I was elated. Then I heard a strange sound coming from her. It was so quiet that I wasn't sure what I'd heard. Had it come from Juliet? I leaned down once more, this time to test it out. I kissed her. There was the sound again. She was growling.

My head popped up. I was shocked, but not hurt as I had been by Todd. This one I sympathized with.

It had been such a tiny, baby growl, I'd almost missed it. In her own sweet, enduring way, she was saying, "I don't like this. I feel trapped."

It's times like these when I'm jarred back into reality—Juliet is not my baby—she's a dog. When Juliet came to us, I held her in much the same way I had held my own babies as they drifted off to sleep on my chest and stayed that way until they woke up so that I could be there to welcome them back. On an unconscious level, I knew that Juliet's purpose with me was healing the rift with my family, as Duke, the messenger, had foretold. But she was not here to be another child. She wants to be a dog.

It is fitting that I should have conceived of the idea of bringing a Bernese Mountain Dog into our family at a Shakespeare in the Park play, swords, castles, honor, family. In a previous life together, Juliet and I had a similar relationship to the one we share today. At that time, I had a knowledge of healing herbs. And she had been a great defender of boundaries, a modern day soldier, a knight. At a time when she needed me, I was able to heal her.

One night, a great battle had taken place. Our fortress was assaulted on all sides. Many knights were wounded that day. My assistants and I had our work cut out for us. By firelight in the straw-strewn floor of that castle, we worked tirelessly into the night to heal the wounded and help ease the discomfort of the dying. Juliet's soul had been among them. Looking into my eyes that night, she vowed to me as she lay dying that she would not let any harm come to me, she would protect me.

After Brittney's death, I knew even before Juliet arrived that hers would be just as agonizing for me. Only now, another dimension to that had opened up. I can see a new aspect to that inevitable day when I'll reluctantly say goodbye to Juliet. The word dread doesn't do my feelings justice. It puts it on par with something like going to the dentist. So like so many other times in my life, words fail me. But if I had to equate the feeling to something, it would be fear. I choose fear because somewhere deep in my soul there is still that memory of that day centuries ago when I'd been unable to save another soul's life. That fear motivates me to protect her health so fiercely today, even knowing all along that her years with me are limited.

Juliet's soul kept her dying promise to protect me, even sending Duke ahead of her to remind me of the promise she'd made that terrible night. *Healing.* She was reminding me of what I'd been to her. That had been my life's purpose. And that was the very thing she wanted to return to me—healing through her protection.

In the great Shakespeare work Romeo and Juliet, the Montagues and the Capulets reconcile after the deaths of their beloved children, Romeo and Juliet. When Montague contemplates erecting a statue in honor of Juliet, he says, "There shall no figure at such rate be set as that of true and faithful Juliet."

Our Juliet is named for that beloved character, and she is also responsible for my reconciliation with my parents.

Six years before had been the first time I had as an adult asserted my independence from my parents. Pregnant with my daughter, I was twenty-eight years old and had endured a lifetime of trampling over my personal boundaries. My son was three, the age from which I had my first memory. All I could see in him was light and love, not the inherited sinful nature that I had been accused of having. I needed to protect both of my children and in doing so, protect the young girl I had been. And unfortunately, a total break was the only way I saw that would be possible. I spent the next six years learning about myself in therapy, reading, and trying to put my past into perspective. It was during this time that my anxiety reached its peak without my family of origin and part of the reason I had reincarnated in the first place. But through therapy, I was able to not only discover that I had done nothing to deserve my parents' treatment but was also able to feel real anger towards them, without guilt. Today, I feel compassion for the place they must have been emotionally.

Finally, I came out of those years realizing that my early experiences had made me who I am today. And my experiences and of course my choices had led me to the place I found myself. I have a wonderful husband, my best friend. I have two children who are light to my soul, my teachers. I have a house full of animal friends and laughter and love. For all of that, I could not be angry.

But I have been forced to come to terms with my own pain, to find a way to live with it. That was the choice I had to make, to find a different way of looking at my life. I discovered that comparing my pain to other people's either diminished my experiences in my mind (and that's not fair) or it caused me to hold tighter to the pain. Every person's path is different for a reason, and I may not understand the reasons for my experiences until my journey has come to an end and I can look back on my life with 20/20 hindsight.

My daughter was six years old when I knew it was time to reconcile with my parents. She was old enough to tell me if she ever felt violated, and I was ready to heal.

Juliet was the catalyst for the letter I wrote my dad. She was with us when as a family we returned to my parents' house.

Juliet coming to me made all of this possible.

Dogs are one thing that my mother and I have always both loved. We can talk for hours about them. I wrote to my parents, told them that I needed to set some clear boundaries. They agreed, saying that they realized that all three of their children were different. And if they wanted relationship with them, they would have to accept that. I celebrated that letter.

When I wrote back, I told them about Juliet, our little puppy who looked just like a stuffed animal. I wanted my parents to meet her.

My family and I took her with us to my parents' house to celebrate Thanksgiving that year. I know now as I realized that day through the tears in my eyes, that my parents had done the best they could with what they had, as we all do every day. That's all we can do. And that's all we can expect.

Juliet's purpose in coming to me was to express herself, all of her emotions actually. In a previous incarnation, her family, the knighthood she had belonged to, while a central part of her life, was bound by duty, not emotion. But today, Juliet is expressive of everything she feels. She barks (loudly) when she is happy, mad, curious, or hurt. She won't let anyone sit alone. She makes sure that she presses against you, sometimes to the detriment of your balance. And she will shovel your hand until you pet her. And once you start, if you stop petting her, she will pop back up and make you start over. She is one of the most communicative dogs I have ever known. She even talks to her vet. And luckily for us, he hears her.

She also has very clear boundaries, something that I still struggle with. So she is my teacher. I prefer situations and people that flow. For that reason, the reason my children call me diplomatic, I chose to bring a Bernese Mountain Dog into our family, a benignant and gentle breed. I wanted a family dog and I got one. Juliet is simply put, kind. But that doesn't mean that she doesn't express her boundaries very clearly to the delivery truck drivers who appear at our home, uninvited as far as she is concerned. And she expresses her boundaries to me. She knows herself, what she likes, and what she doesn't. She didn't worry that she would offend the stranger on the beach who had encroached on her personal space and mine. And she encourages me to know myself in the same way.

By healing the break in my relationship with my parents, Juliet was able to heal herself. Since her purpose here on Earth was to bring my family together with her expression of love, she fulfilled the dying vow she had made to me.

Thanks to Juliet keeping her promise, my parents and I share a relationship based on mutual respect of boundaries today. I believe in my heart that if my parents had a chance to do things differently in this life, they would. Today, I know that they would do anything for me and my family. My mother's recent Thanksgiving card said how they thank God for me and my husband and children. I do the same. I also thank God for second chances to learn, grow, and improve. I also thank God for the way my mother keeps surprising me, all because I gave us a second chance. Do we still have karma we're working out together? You can be sure of it. And for that, because of our willingness to come back together in this life and get better, it's a relationship worth having. I got my mother back. Is our relationship perfect? No, but it's ours. Our relationship was worth salvaging. We need each other; we wouldn't have come back together if we hadn't. Working through difficulties that cause us to feel disconnected from the sacred part of ourselves is, I believe, our purpose here on Earth. In reconnecting with the Divine, I found my purpose.

If my parents had not been who they'd promised to be, I might not fully appreciate the blessings I have as I look around the dinner table at the faces there. My son, my daughter, my husband, and the love we share with our furry friends are the best things in my life. If I had grown up in any other way with any other people, I might not truly *get* that.

I don't think I'll fully understand the import of

Come Back

Juliet's presence in my life until I can look back on my time with her, with 20/20 hindsight, as they say. Until then, a time my heart dreads, I know that her purpose with me is significant beyond words.

Until then, I know that she is in my life to help defend me and my boundaries. She has the heart of a knight who promises to defend the vulnerable. In return for her protection, I take good care of her. I make sure that she gets natural foods and holistic care.

From the first time I held her in Asheville, North Carolina, the day we brought her home, and she licked my chin, it was love at first sight for both of us.

Juliet continues to be a source of great happiness and familial harmony for me, my husband, and my children. She reminds us on a daily basis how important it is to express ourselves like she does, "I don't like that" or "I love you" and "I'm so happy to see you".

She's great at setting boundaries.

Tina Proffitt

14.
Daisy, Scotch, and Roger's Story

Come Back

Roger and my daughter

Neighbors and Friends

Daisy was a green-eyed pure white-haired beauty who lived in the cul-de-sac one street down from ours. My daughter, my son, my husband, and I took Juliet on regular walks through our neighborhood. My daughter was six when Juliet came into our lives. By the time Juliet was full grown, my daughter had begun to tell me of ways she talked to animals. One day on one of our walks while we looked for one of our favorite things, mushroom rings or fairy rings as we referred to them, I asked her how she talked to animals. She said that she imagined what she wanted to ask like it was a drawing on a piece of paper. Then she imagined sliding the piece of paper to the animal. Little did I know at the time, but would soon find out at my animal communication class, that was exactly how animals communicate with one another, through visual images, mental pictures. And my daughter knew how to do this without anyone ever teaching her.

I began my animal communication classes that summer and as the days grew hotter and hotter our walks began earlier and earlier in the day. On one particular morning we'd gotten a late start and decided to take a short walk. As we made our way down the cul-de-sac next to ours, a beautiful pure white cat appeared from the house on the corner. At this time, my daughter did not have a cat of her own and quickly became enamored of this one. Juliet sat down on the side of the road and waited for us to continue. My daughter squatted down and began talking to the cat.

Over time, each time we stopped, the cat in response rubbed her face on the bumper of her owner's Jeep. Then she came closer, rubbing her face on the mailbox. Eventually, she was close enough for my daughter to reach out and stroke her back. I joined in too.

On subsequent walks, we discovered this cat's name was Daisy and according to her owners, she never let any strangers touch her. My daughter must be special, they said. I agreed. As the months passed, we had it confirmed by Daisy's next door neighbor that indeed we must be cat whisperers because Daisy did not venture down to the end of her driveway for anyone else. We felt honored and privileged to be trusted by Daisy.

As I learned more and more about communication from my animal classes, I decided to test my new skill with Daisy. I determined to ask her a question I could get a concrete answer to. And one day as we paused in front of her house to say hello, I sent her a question. I asked what her favorite spot to sleep was in her house. I received a ready answer. A picture of an orange-colored recliner. Then not a week later on another one of our walks, I saw there on the driveway of Daisy's house, an old orange-colored recliner sitting in the back of the owner's truck getting ready to be donated. Wow! I thought. I hadn't made it up. I had received a message from a cat. Even better, I'd got it right. Now, if only I could tell her owners, without freaking them out, that that was Daisy's favorite chair they were about to give away.

In Biblical times, there was a seven-year famine in Egypt. The Nile River had dried up and the people starved. During this time, Daisy and I lived there together. We had been neighbors then too. She had been very beautiful and prized for her beauty. Yet she lived a life that lacked substance. It was only when the famine worsened and our families too became hungry that we realized that our lives would soon end. None of our families survived the famine. And we, as young people, died without ever fulfilling our hopes or dreams. I still carry the soul memory of this with me even today whenever I fear that there might not be enough food to go around or that I might die before fulfilling my hopes and dreams.

From us, Daisy was able to discern for herself without a doubt that there is indeed abundance in the universe, enough love to go around. Every time we stopped to talk to Daisy, we showed her that the street upon which she lived was not just full of dogs that wanted to chase her, noisy cars and trucks that scared her, and people that didn't have time for her. We showed her that she was worth our time just because of who she was.

Growing up, my mother would always say to me, "pretty is as pretty does," meaning that beauty comes from the inside of a person not just the outside. I thought it was just a simple admonition not to be vain. But now I see the truth in the words. When we live our life knowing that there is enough for everyone, we need not worry. We can focus on the things that truly matter. Not only was Daisy a beautiful cat, she had beauty inside as well, and she was able to share it with us, her neighbors.

Scotch was a toffee and black cat with a big personality. He literally stopped us on a bike ride through our neighborhood one day. My daughter was small and still fit into the trailer I had attached to my bike, the same bike my husband and I bought for trail riding on our honeymoon to Pisgah National Forest. My son rode his bike and the three of us would set out for our morning exercise before we started our lessons.

Our first meeting with Scotch, we didn't know that a cat even lived on this particular street. Our neighborhood sits right next to another older neighborhood with bigger houses. So this was one of our cut-through streets that took us back home. There was a big hill and once we'd reached the top of it, we would sometimes stop for a sip or two of water before setting off for home. This particular day, the wind blew across our heated bodies and we heard a cry. It sounded at first like a small child. We knew that the house we'd stopped in front of had small children. My husband

Come Back

who's a huge Landcruiser fan had said that another member of the Landcruiser club lived in that house and they had children. But eventually, a beautiful cat appeared, meowing at us as if to say, "Hello, there you are. I've been waiting for you." On subsequent trips, we discovered from a neighbor across the street that the cat's name was Scotch and to watch out because he was a biter. So far though, we'd petted him and talked to him and had not been bitten. We never picked him up. Most cats don't enjoy being held outdoors where there are so many dangers they may need to run away from at any second. So my kids and I knew better. So I thanked him for the introduction.

One particular Monday morning as we rode up to Scotch's house and stopped as had become our habit, we called for him, and as usual here he came running up to us. I still recall the charge I got from our visits with Scotch. He was talkative and demonstrative. He just had a way of making you feel like his friend. And by then, he had developed a way of greeting us, each in turn. After saying hello to my son on his bike first, he would come to the trailer where my daughter sat next, then finally to the front of my bike. He would stretch up to me, claws out, and blink at me. I loved it. On this day, as he stretched, I reached down to scratch the top of his head. He closed his eyes and suddenly lost his balance. In a momentary panic, he reached out for something to stop him from falling over and grabbed my right hand. His very sharp claws dug into the soft flesh of my palm. My hand instantly began to bleed and I realized that with a good twenty-minute bike ride still ahead of us and no first aid kit, I'd better get home and clean my hand. With a quick goodbye to Scotch, we left him there in the street looking after us.

We took our rides three times a week, so we didn't come back until Wednesday morning. And instead of us having to call Scotch as we'd become accustomed to doing, there he sat on the curb waiting for us. Instead of greeting my children first, he came straight to me, meowing. I knew he was asking about my hand. He walked straight to my hand sniffed it, and instead of stretching up to me, which had landed me with a scratched hand in the first place, he rubbed his head on my bandage. I told him that it had not been his fault and all was forgotten. But I left that morning with a profound sense of relationship with Scotch. Such a deliberate display of caring from a cat might have been lost on me had I not been paying attention.

In the months to come, Scotch would move on to another home. According to his owners, he had just shown up at their house one day and about a year later he was gone. They had later discovered that Scotch had moved in with a family on the next street. According to my husband's friend, the other house served better food. So although we continued for several weeks to call Scotch, we never saw him again. He, like all great performers, left us wanting more.

Our paths had crossed before, Scotch's and mine. And in our previous life together, Scotch had been the victim of an abusive uncle. Because of this, he learned to do as he was told without question. Therefore, he did not lead the life he wished for. In this life, Scotch is learning to live life on his own terms. He refuses to be tied to one family, instead choosing to move from family to family, learning all he can about relationships in the short years he has on Earth.

Come Back

Scotch knew that I was just starting out on my journey to commune with animals and coming to a place of understanding our relationships with one another. And he was instrumental in showing me how much care and concern can be expressed through a small creature who is sometimes overlooked and sometimes grossly misunderstand in comparison because he doesn't wag his tail.

Roger was another cat we had the pleasure of meeting on our bike rides. He was large, sleek, and black with green eyes, like a panther. We met Roger in the cul-de-sac up from Daisy's house. Our first meeting with Roger, he approached us on our way home. And not only did he thoroughly rub against each of our legs, when he was done he jumped right into the trailer along with my daughter (pictured). She laughed and giggled as he got into her lap, thrilled that he, a stranger, would get so close. It was a cold day and we'd brought along a fleece blanket for her to wear. Roger snuggled right into her lap on top of that blanket. I'll never forget sensing that he really wanted to go for a ride. We knew from a neighbor that he lived in the small house on that corner along with three kids and two very large dogs, a Doberman Pinscher and a Great Dane who shared a twenty by twenty-foot back yard enclosed by a three-foot chain length fence. The Doberman would stand on his hind legs with his front legs propped on the fence top and bark as people passed his yard.

We made it a regular part of our bike ride to stop, and we looked forward to saying hello to Roger in the same spot across the street from his house in a little culvert area on top of a storm drain. And every morning, he would hop into the trailer with my daughter. When we were ready to go, I would have to lift him out and say goodbye. I felt he really did want to go with us.

One morning, Roger wasn't there. As I'd had some practice with animal communication by then, I tried asking Roger where he was. He showed me a car and the feeling that he had moved. I gathered that because he was such a friendly cat, he eventually was picked up. He'd certainly willingly gotten into our bike trailer enough times. I was informed by a neighbor that Roger's owners did not know where he was. I felt so sad at the loss of Roger from mine and my children's lives.

I know now that Roger had needed to move on. In a previous life, he had been in prison. He could not stay inside his house without feeling extremely panicked. He only felt safe out in the open. Part of his purpose in coming to Earth as a cat was to roam. And roam, he did. We are not the only ones to miss Roger. But he is living the life that he needed to live for his soul's growth. He needed to experience life through travel.

Happy trails, Roger.

We miss you! And we'll never forget you.

15.
Susan's Story

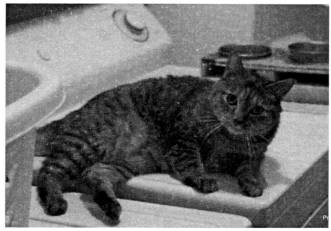

Susie

Mirror, Mirror

My parents' fear that I would somehow turn out bad without their intervention, that I had not been *born* good enough, became my fear that I could never *be* good enough.

When we are born, we all contain just enough fear to keep us by our parents' sides until we are older and ready to explore. But for me, that fear became magnified. My brain's perception of what was safe and what wasn't was warped. My normal amount of apprehension became an abnormal amount, to the point of not feeling safe unless I was with my parents. Today I only feel truly safe when I am at my home. My normal amount of anxiety became an uncontrollable amount of fear to the point of not feeling safe in the world, something with which I still struggle today. I am

Come Back

happiest at home, being productive, where I can love my family, and take good care of my body and mind. But I don't like to leave the house. In fact, I have to take herbs just to get in the car.

Susan, or Susie as she's called now, a beautiful brown and black tabby, was named by the humane society. My daughter was finally able to pick out a cat of her own. She bypassed the room full of adorable kittens. She instead wanted a more grown-up cat. Susie was curled into a ball in the corner of her cage. She did not get up or meow at my daughter, but nevertheless drew her in like a tractor beam.

Across the room, I found a friendly cat who had obviously just had a litter of kittens and my heart went out to her. I called my daughter over.

"Just come look at her," I pleaded.

But my daughter wouldn't budge. She had made up her mind. She had found her soulmate. Susie was her choice.

Susie didn't squirm or move much at all when my daughter scooped her up. We would later learn that this was due to the sedative medicine still in her system. Susie had recently been spayed. Her stitches were still fresh. Nevertheless, I recognized that love-at-first-sight look in my daughter's eyes.

We brought Susie home in a travel crate. By the time we got there, the medicine had burned off considerably, and Susie was wide-eyed with fear. Never before had I seen a cat so traumatized. For weeks, she didn't move from the back of the crate. She ate, slept, and did everything else in there. Every day, I would change out the newspaper, the water, add food to her bowl, hoping to make contact with her. But she remained afraid of me, of her new world.

About a month went by and my daughter had made it a daily ritual to visit Susie at her crate. She would sit in front of the open door, talk to her, coax her to come out. And finally, one day, a triumphant voice came from the room. "She let me hold her!"

I was shocked. But there my daughter was, holding this cat who had barely moved in two months. I was so happy that I ran for the camera. That is one of my favorite pictures. She had done it. She had slowly but surely taught Susie that this was a safe world that she had entered. No more surgery, no more strangers, she was safe now.

Susie was such a mystery to us. The shelter did not have a history on her. At four months of age, she was dropped off as a stray. But through my communication with Susie, I discovered that she had lived under a shed-type building from the time she was born. She had stayed there in hiding with her brothers and sisters, venturing only to the edge of the structure for food from a kind stranger, a human. Eventually, she and her brothers had been trapped by this human and taken to the humane society.

To this day, Susie is afraid of people wearing shoes, especially my husband's work boots. She is still a very cautious cat, preferring the space between the wall and the washer and dryer as her safety zone. We even keep an extra bed for her back there. But she ventures out every day to greet us, to eat, to be held, brushed, and petted by my daughter. She even braves the screened porch.

She and my daughter have a special history together of being sisters in a monastery. Their souls have finally reunited together again in a different form of sisterhood.

In yet another incarnation, Susie told me about being governess to two children. I have often compared our home school to being like the work of an old-fashioned governess. In that life, Susie had been afraid of the man of the house, her charges' father. He would come home from hunting, wearing heavy boots. His loud footsteps had echoed through the great hall of the home, and she had known he was headed upstairs to question her about his children's studies, to see if she performed up to par for him.

Today, she is able to safely be with us while we study. Her soul can relive that life she lived previously, comfortably now. She only has to sit back and close her eyes, listening to our school lessons instead of being responsible for them.

In a previous life with me, Susie was a writer and I was her father. In this previous incarnation together, Susie wrote about her spirituality. As a nun, she was blessed with ample time to reflect upon life and the teachings of spirit.

In this life, I have chosen to teach my children at home and write books that have mysticism woven into them. It is as though, we have reversed our previous roles, but we are still repeating them. Practice makes perfect. But my books are not purely spiritual. They are mystical romance novels inspired by the books I love to read, books about the reuniting of souls from past lifetimes. I find so much hope in this way of viewing the world. Our relationships are continuous. Although I mourn, I never have to feel that I have lost anyone completely to death. Our souls can come together again.

Tina Proffitt

Beginning my writing career, independently publishing romance novels online, was fraught with pitfalls. I experienced a great deal of fear. Mostly my fears revolved around exposing parts of myself. If all art is self-portraiture, including the written word, then what I wrote would allow readers to see inside of me to the secret parts I kept hidden from the rest of the world. I didn't know if I wanted that.

Like Susie, there was a part of me that wanted to find a small space between the wall and the washer and dryer to hide.

My inner-gypsy, the part of my soul that longs to wander, frightens me. The drive in my car to one of the animal communication classes several summers ago began my daily struggle with leaving my house. This particular class was held out of town at another member's home and in an unfamiliar city. On the way there, I panicked. I wanted to go home. Fortunately, I had herbs in my purse and was able to press on. Since then, I've come to realize that I had gotten so close to my purpose that fear raised its ugly head. I think that's the way it is when I come up against that thing that I am here on Earth for—my fear threatens to prevent me.

As Dr. Darren Weissman said, "Remember when excitement and fear meet at a crossroads, you know that you're on the precipice of a life transformation."

In a previous life, I had been a Bard, a man who traveled from community to community, stopping long enough to eat and tell my stories and make friends. Unfortunately, at one stop I made in Brittany (the place for which I named Brittney without being consciously aware of it), a man and a woman got in my way. The man was the owner of the land. The woman he loved fell in love with me. As punishment for my perceived wrong against him, the rich land owner falsely accused me of stealing a piece of valuable jewelry from him and had me imprisoned. I died three years later of a broken heart in that prison. So you can see why my fear is triggered by traveling too far from home in this my current life.

But I didn't let my fear stop me from continuing those animal communication classes. I attended every meeting for the rest of that summer. I needed that class. I had to learn to communicate with the animals if I was going to fulfill a part of my life's purpose—writing the book in your hands.

I've asked myself many times why I needed to be out in the world if I was happier right where I was in my safe little cocoon, like Susie.

Publishing my books however, putting my thoughts out there, became my way of going out into the world. In my books, I unleash my inner-gypsy woman. For now, she is confined to my books and I'm okay with that. Instead of physically becoming a nomad, something I could never do to my children who I want to provide stability, I use the written word to explore my world.

Like me, Susie had a difficult childhood that had taught her to fear the world. And because of this, Susie became my mirror. Cats are independent, so am I. Cats are extremely cautious, so am I. Susie slowly but surely everyday tests the waters of her boundaries, so do I. Occasional setbacks send Susie back into hiding, as they do me. But today I use herbal remedies for anxiety that do wonders for my body and remind me that I have all the resources I need available to me, provided to me by Mother Nature. I need not be afraid.

Susie's lessons this time are to overcome her fears. I cannot think of a more efficient way of doing that than choosing to incarnate as a feral cat who finds her way into a family of people who love her and want to see her embrace her life. Yet Susie does not feel ashamed of her fear. She doesn't let it ruin her self-esteem like I had.

Fear has its lessons for me if I will hear it. Just as peace and joy tell me that I am feeding my soul, fear tells me that I have come up against something that a part of me is not ready to accept. So as much as I would like to live without fear, I do not try to lose my fear or eradicate it—I try to embrace it. Fear is temporary. It is fleeting like every other emotion. When fear rears its ugly head, I turn to it and say, *what do I need to know?* Peace is not the absence of fear any more than happiness is the absence of sadness. How many times have I laughed as I cried? Peace is simply a deep, inner knowing that all things work together for good—that no matter what, all will be well.

Like Susie's early-life fear of the world, the same could be said of me and my early life. I came into this world through a family that lived in fear. But I eventually found my way to my husband. Our souls found each other just as we agreed before coming to Earth. He wants to see me embrace my life.

I choose not to let my fear stop me from doing what I am here on Earth to do. As we all do, I've got a light inside of me that shouldn't be kept hidden under a bushel. Every day, I choose to sit down at my laptop and write. I have a lot of things inside me that I have yet to say.

Come Back

Every soul I cross paths with has shown up as promised, allowing challenges to become my lessons. Whether it's being bitten by a dog, or scared by a runaway horse, or being afraid to leave my safe spot, I can view all of my relationships as opportunities to learn. Every day I can look into the mirror that my animals hold in front of me and ask, "What do I need to know today?"

Tina Proffitt

Conclusion

Come Back

What I've Learned Along the Way

Back to that fateful day in November when I made a choice that would irrevocably change my life. Without even asking the woman on the pavement if she was okay, I sprinted across all six lanes of traffic. I had sprinted for the track team in school, my one and only claim to physical intelligence. My only thought was one—catch up to the little brown dog. I watched his or her body dart into the trees of the undeveloped land across the street. I barely noticed the car that screeched to a stop because there was a *person* running across the road.

Brightly colored leaves lay on the dormant, yellow grass. The ground, having been shaded from the morning sun, was still wet from the previous night's dew.

I lost sight of the little brown dog in the undergrowth. I tried calling him. "Here, doggie!"

But he was nowhere to be seen. Then as if having just materialized out of nothing, another woman appeared, not the woman I had seen fall face first across the street. And she called the dog by name. *How did she get here?* I thought.

I had not seen her cross the street. I didn't even know there had been another woman. But there she was. Now my entire purpose in risking my life collapsed around me. *What had I been thinking?* That dog wasn't going to come near me, a stranger, in his panicked state.

In an instant, all of my adrenaline left me. I deflated like an old birthday balloon. I knew that I had crossed that busy street, risked life and limb for a stranger's dog, and it had all been for nothing. My help hadn't even been needed in the first place.

Returning to my truck was a much trickier situation than going had been. For one, I wasn't chasing after a runaway dog, no adrenaline. For another, there was still that blind curve at the top of a hill. Only this time, I was inside the curve. It rounded in front of the vet's clinic, making it impossible for cars coming towards me to see me this time until it was too late.

I waited for an opening like Frogger. And this time my own safety *was* a consideration. I bolted across the street, making it safely across for the second time.

I returned to my truck in daze, unlocking the door.

What did I just do? I repeated over and over in my mind.

The injured woman was back on her feet now. I heard her speaking to me as I unlocked my truck.

"Thank you," she said.

I turned to her. "I'm sorry that happened to you."

What I'd wanted to say was that I knew how bereft I would have been if it had been Juliet running from me. (I had been in those shoes before.) And I wanted to say that I was sorry that my effort had not helped.

I fell into the driver's seat, slumping into a heap of loose muscles and bones. I hung my head.

"I'm so sorry, guys," I said to my children, patiently waiting for me in the backseat.

"For what?" they chorused.

"For doing something so dangerous. I should never have run across that street."

"It's okay, Mommy," they both said.

With tears streaming down my cheeks, I shook my head. "No, no it's not really. I risked my life. And that's not smart. I'm your mommy, and that's too important to be so careless."

I'm sure my children did not fully realize the import of my words that day. Someday if they have children of their own, they might look back on that day and realize what I meant. But I felt that I owed them an apology.

I wanted to tell my husband what had happened right away, to call him at work from the truck and cry. I needed that. But I knew my husband, a firefighter, a man who'd made a career of putting his life in danger for others for the past twenty-five years, would not like it if I told him what I had done. I knew his motto, *you can't help anybody if you you're dead.*

So I didn't. Instead I swallowed my cowardice. And I kept my secret for the next four years.

I did tell one person during that time though, my therapist, Judy.

"When I got back into the truck," I said to her one day in her office, "a terrible realization crashed down on me. I began to cry because I realized how wrong it had been to run across that street."

Judy had simply shaken her head. "Everyone who's done something heroic feels guilt afterward when they realize that what they did was dangerous. You simply did what any hero would do. You acted selflessly."

Selfless. Putting another person's needs ahead of mine, that wasn't so bad. I did that every day as a mother. But I categorically refuted the label of hero. But selfless, that was good. I could live with that one. But I still didn't tell my husband. I pride myself on being responsible. And this would prove me otherwise.

I did eventually tell my husband—but not until

recently—before I sat down to write this book as a matter of fact. I owed him that much. I had carried my secret around with me for four years, wincing every time I thought about my sprint across those six lanes of traffic.

I was ready to come clean.

After all was said and done, I found that I had nothing to worry about. My husband took my story well. In fact, he was wonderful about it. Apparently, he did know a thing or two about regret. Twenty-five years in a dangerous profession had landed him in some tight spots too. And he recognized that I had been beating myself up over the choice I had made.

"I replay the scene in my mind," I said to him that night in our bedroom. I had been on my way into the bathroom to take a shower when I realized I had to tell him. "And every time I do, I can't imagine not going across that street. I couldn't have just heedlessly gotten into my truck and driven off, safe and sound, with that woman just lying there. I made the only choice I could live with."

He nodded. "Everyone has to make the choice they know they can live with."

"But I don't trust myself anymore," I cried. "I'm afraid I'll run right out into traffic again and not be so lucky the next time."

This was not the first time I'd lost my head over a runaway dog. Living in a neighborhood full of family dogs, most of them spending their days in backyards while their owners earn a living, means that some of them eventually find a way out of that yard. Locating the slightest hole in the fence with which to squeeze out, they take off on an adventure, sometimes through my

Come Back

front yard. I've been known to keep a sandwich baggie of treats and a leash by the front door for just such occasions.

Still my husband shook his head. "Every situation has options. Instead of beating yourself up, ask yourself what you could do differently next time."

"Okay."

"What could you have done differently if the same thing happened all over again?"

"I could ask the woman if she was okay first."

"Okay. What else?"

"If I had spoken to her, I would've found out that she had a friend with her who was going after the dog."

"Exactly. You can make a different choice."

I breathed a sigh of relief. *Why hadn't I thought of that?*

Perhaps if I had rescued the little dog that day, my question of *why* I'd done it would have ended there—I'd have saved a dog. But I didn't, which made it all the harder for me to sit with. I'd risked my life, and for what? That question led me to ask even more of myself, like how my choices had led me to where I found myself and how my future choices would affect me. A lot of fear followed those questions.

In our family, raising our kids, my husband and I have put a lot of emphasis on making choices. Everything comes down to our personal choices, we teach our kids. When they were little, we were very big on personal responsibility. And not just picking out their own clothes, we encouraged that too, like those numerous occasions that I was escorted to the library or to the grocery store by a miniature princess or Batman, cape and all. But we encouraged the big choices like how to treat others. We tried to teach our children that making choices involved all aspects of life. Because isn't that what our daily life all really comes down to, choices?

When we see someone making a choice we wouldn't make, we say, as long as they're not hurting themselves or others, *that's their choice*.

I choose what time I go to bed at night, before or after another TV show. I choose whether I will take good care of my teeth. I choose what time to wake up in the morning, giving myself plenty of time to make it to work or just enough. I choose what kind of food I'll start my day with, something that will feed my body or something that will simply tempt my palette. I can choose my attitude for the day.

When it comes down to it, no one can make my choices for me. Even choosing to allow others to make them for me is another choice.

In our house, we have another saying, "That's your choice." It means that no one can "make" you do anything. Everything's a choice.

And at the end of life, aren't most people reflecting upon the lifetime of choices they've made?

So I continued for the rest of the evening to mull over what Scott had said. I realized that I didn't have to fear anymore that I was somehow a loose cannon who couldn't be trusted with the safety and responsibility of my own life. Next time, I could make a *different choice*, one that I could live with. And that didn't have to mean that I would become Frogger again.

And so...

That is what I believe life is all about, doing our best to get it right no matter how long it takes, no matter how many tries.

Sin is something I heard a lot about growing up. In fact, I recall one particular private school that had written on the wall of the auditorium in giant letters a verse from Romans, "For the wages of sin is death," a big pill for a little kid to swallow. But the word sin is also an archery term, meaning "off the mark". I have taught my children that sin is anything that isn't in our best interest. Looking back, I can see now why all those sermons I'd listened to as a kid cautioned me not to smoke or drink or use drugs or gamble. These things would side-track my life of its purpose. In tarot, the devil card represents those things in our life that side-track us from our purpose, move us *off the mark.*

If you were to ask my children, "how do we learn?", they would answer with one of my favorite refrains, "by making mistakes".

As a teacher and homeschool mother, I know the truth of that all too well. I learn best through my mistakes. And I have tried to make sure my children know that.

There are two words from the Bible that showed up quite often in my childhood, good and evil. Translated from the original language, we find that the word for good meant ripe. And the word for evil translated to unripe. Big difference! One piece of fruit is ready to eat. One isn't. We do not judge a piece of fruit for not being ready to eat. We do not say to the fruit, "You are evil because you're green." Why then should we judge ourselves?

And after the judging comes the sentencing.

I do not believe that a difficult life is punishment for wrong-doings in past lives, on the contrary.

Tina Proffitt

Struggling means we are growing, living the life we are meant to live. Judy would say you can only get a diamond from intense heat and pressure.

When our kids were little, my husband and I did not use punishment. Instead we employed natural consequences. If you made a mess, you cleaned it up. If you knocked someone down, you helped them back up. If you knocked down another person's block tower, you built it back up. To this day as teenagers who have their normal squabbles, when things get overheated, we sit down as a family to mirror and validate the feelings from which the unconscious behaviors sprang. That way we can find the source of the original problem. And believe me, sitting across the table from sometimes long-winded parents for an hour can at times feel like punishment to them.

But just as a lump of coal must undergo a tremendous amount of heat and pressure before the diamond can be created, it is the same with our souls. We choose to live lives that will squeeze and hurt, transforming us into that beautiful diamond, that divine spark, inside us.

In this light, trials and pain can never be seen as a punishment from an angry God. On the contrary, the path to achieve oneness, the return to the bosom of the divine, is fraught with challenges so that we might improve. Just as Frodo had to come near to death to return the ring to its source, or Harry Potter had to die in order to defeat Voldemort, or Luke Skywalker had to lose his home, his parents, his aunt and uncle, and his hand in order to defeat the Emperor, we too must suffer in order to return to our source.

My fear of getting life wrong, of making mistakes,

of not being good enough, has in the past caused me to fear death. Death is rapidly becoming a less and less scary notion, at least in my eyes.

As Socrates, the Greek stonemason and philosopher once said, "A man who is good for anything ought not to calculate the chance of living or dying; he ought only to consider whether in doing anything he is doing right or wrong—acting the part of a good man or a bad.... For the fear of death is indeed the pretense of wisdom, but a pretense of knowing the unknown; and no one knows whether death, which men in their fear apprehend to be the greatest evil, may not be the greatest good."

I take comfort in his words that death is not something to be feared.

"Death is nothing to be afraid of," Judy said to me one evening over the phone. I'd just whispered to her that I was afraid of dying, so that my daughter, a toddler at the time, and son, playing in the other room, wouldn't overhear. "Bodies are like cars," she went on to say. "When we crash them, sometimes we need another one. But our souls remain intact. Death is just like taking off a pair of too-tight shoes at the end of a long day—relief."

But what of the after? I thought. Did God, like my English 201 professor, give me just enough rope to run with or hang myself with? I still answer my fears with a resounding, *No*, at least, not in the sense that I'd been led to believe.

Perhaps I can sum up my views on this with a metaphor.

Have you ever played on a team (I haven't, but my husband taught me everything I know about being a team player) with a coach who really cared about you? If you have, you may have experienced the after-loss speech. As I have already admitted, I am not athletic, unless you count being able to run really fast between point A and point B, but not for long without a knee brace or developing shin splints. So I have never been on the receiving end of this speech personally. But I did grow up in a family with two siblings, my older brother and younger sister, who were both exceptional athletes. So, I spent a lot of my spare time on the bleachers, on the sidelines, and at the end-of-the-season trophy ceremony. As a result, I heard my fair share of pep-talks, not that I appreciated them at the time any more than my siblings appreciated my straight A report cards. But in hindsight, I see their value.

Please indulge me as I give my own version of one now. Imagine me pacing with a clip board in hand, whistle around my neck if it helps.

"They were a tough team. We never expected to win; they were undefeated. But we went out there and did our best. Why? Because we had to, that's why. We had to prove to ourselves that we could do it. We had to face Goliath, stare him down, and walk away with our heads held high. Now, we've learned a few things we wouldn't have been able to learn any other way. We will keep our heads down, work hard, and start over next season, knowing that we can face any obstacle we encounter. We might not come out victorious, but we will have improved. And as long as you're doing that, you can never lose!"

At the end of a loss, especially if you thought you had it all wrapped up going in, and you got trounced, you have two options. You can pout, of course. You can take it personally. This is what's known as being a sore loser. (I cried when I was rotated out of my first and only volleyball game.) Or you can rehash what happened during the game, see where you went wrong, and make adjustments for next time. In other words, or in the words of my wonderful husband, you can make a *different* choice next time. I didn't need to beat myself up over running into the street after another person's dog. I made a choice, that in the benefit of hindsight, didn't suit me. I could make a different choice next time.

Such is life!

To extend the metaphor even further, some of those players may not return to the team next season. Some, like my brother and sister, will likely be living in another state by then. Some may decide that baseball is not for them and try soccer. Still others may hate basketball but love the coach (the one who encourages them) so much that they will stay with him through baseball season just to be on his team.

So this final pep-talk, and I'm talking on a very grand scale here, as in this judgement day from my childhood, is just that. At the end of our life, when our car has outlived its usefulness, when our bodies have had it, we can return to our place of origin in the bosom of the universe and reassess our lives. We can see where we went wrong and do better next time. That's a lot easier, isn't it? That's what any good coach or loving parent would want for us, isn't it?

I propose another term for judgement—self-evaluation. When used in schools, it can be a powerful motivator for students.

Because I am constantly striving to do my best, to get it right, I chose to reincarnate with those souls that I believed would best help me to accomplish this goal. Thank God I don't have to do this alone. I can look to my neighbors, friends, work associates, family. After all, they all agreed to take my journey with me. And particularly heart-warming is to look into the soulful eyes of my furry, feathered, or scaly friends and know that they are here for the same reason. I have shown up in their lives and they have shown up in mine for the same purpose—to grow together.

So, in closing, if there is a reason why dogs or cats spend only about a decade with us, it could be this—so that they can accomplish a lot in a little amount of time, and so that we can look back on our time with them and see the lessons it held for us. We live so much longer than they, leaving plenty of time and space for us to figure things out.

What a blessing to be able to receive intensive love therapy from another living being who has nowhere else to be but right by our side twenty-four seven. That's a relationship worth having again and again.

I have to trust that what is happening inside me right now is what's supposed to happen. I cannot know why yet because the outcome has not come to pass. All of this, this book, is about 20/20 hindsight and what we can do with it. The healing, as long as we're trusting, will take place, even without our awareness. We need not observe a broken bone to know that it is healing. That is why we can trust that when we do come back, it will be for our highest good and greatest joy. And it will be with souls who've been with us before and want to see us embrace our life.

And we can thank our furry angels for that.

Come Back

Do It Yourself Communication

My own meditation for communicating with animals is very simple. But please keep in mind that you need not conduct readings of your animals in order to heal your past with them.

In India, a country whose citizens largely believe in reincarnation, it is considered by some to be bad luck to ask a child about their previous life. They feel that being aware of too much can only lead to unhappiness in their child's new life.

But because I'm very analytical, I like to know how things got to be the way they are. I think of previous lives in a similar way that I write my novels. I write lots of backstory for the characters I create. There's a whole life that has already occurred that will set the stage for all of their action. I want to know what my characters do for a living, what they eat, what time they like to get up in the morning, even down to what type of vocabulary they use. In a similar way, awareness of previous incarnations can support us in our current life. It can answer the question, what's motivating me? What's behind my behavior or my choices that I'm not aware of?

But you need not know your past in order to heal your future. All you need is the intent to heal. But if you are still interested in delving deeper, begin with the intent to discover that which you *need* to know. And always state that it be for your highest good and greatest joy. That way, the information you receive will be helpful to your healing process.

I always do readings first thing in the morning,

fresh from Heaven, as I used to say of my children. This time of the day works best for me, but if you are interested in starting a practice of your own, I would suggest experimenting with different times of day to find the one that works best for you. Try to find a place where you will be undisturbed for ten or fifteen minutes.

I begin by making sure I am physically very comfortable. I do this in bed under the covers. I stay very still. "Be still and know that I am God." Psalm 46:10.

I keep a notepad beside me for taking notes. I also have my iPod and headphones in case I need some relaxing sounds. This need arises on occasion, like when noisy trucks rumble down my street on garbage collection day.

Next, I ask my angels to surround me and clear my energy of any negative influences, thoughts, or worries that may block information from coming in. My angels include my dog, Brittney, whom I've asked to remain with me in this life, and my guardian angels. Most agree that we have more than one, but I am only consciously aware of one in particular (a human big brother from a previous life) though I feel three human-sized figures total. I ask that the angels belonging to the animal I am reading come in as well. I can also imagine surrounding myself in a protective light, like a bubble.

I usually lay down in a semi-propped up, comfortable position with my muscles relaxed, even my down to my hands, letting them fall loosely at my sides. I take a few deep breaths then center my thoughts on the animal I'm reading. I visualize him or her in my mind or look at a picture that clearly shows the eyes, the windows to the soul. Next, I say my animal's name a few times aloud or in my mind. I can imagine that I'm petting the animal to convey friendship or calm. Now I think of my question. Animals communicate with thought pictures and just by asking the question, I am sending a mental image of what I would like to know. Now I wait. Listen. I may get my answer in the form of a mental image, a feeling, or I may hear words. No matter how I receive the information, it is valid because each individual communicates in his or her own way.

Last, I ask that I be granted permission to read from the Akashic Record anything that I need to know pertaining to a past life of the animal I'm reading.

The Akashic Record, or the Book of Life as it is sometimes called, is according to Edgar Cayce, "God's book of remembrance". It is a memory bank of each individual soul's life, their thoughts, actions, feelings, beliefs, and intent.

So during a reading I will say aloud or silently, for example, "May I receive information that will be for the highest good of all involved about Brittney's previous life with me." In the case of writing this book, this pertained to lives related only to me.

When I do this, I imagine I am in a Greek-style building made of white stone with high pillars in front. There are lots of green plants and sunlight. There are usually robed people milling about inside and out like in a grand library. The Book of Life sits on a pedestal in a place of honor and is already open to the page I need.

What I need to know comes to me in the form of pictures, feelings, and sometimes spoken words. At this point, I just let it come. I take whatever I get (this is not exact science) sometimes writing as I go. And when I feel I have received everything, I thank the angels that surround the book, my angels, and the animal's angels for their assistance.

Sometimes information that comes in won't make sense immediately or ever. In those cases, I just have to trust. Most often, I will think for the rest of the day about what I have received. By the next morning, things will sometimes make more sense. In writing this book, I discovered connections between me and my animals that surprised me at first, but in most cases, after I thought about them for a while, made perfect sense.

You may find that you too are surprised by what you discover. But don't get discouraged. Messages from Spirit can be astounding, but they are always helpful. And once you get started, you may find that you want to know more about every animal you've ever known. I like to think of this as my energetic to-do list. Once I discover what I need to know to heal one relationship, I want to do more and more. And each time I do this, each time I check off another name from my list, I can rest assured that it will be for the highest good of all involved.

It is my sincerest hope that you too will find answers, inspiration, and hope for your future from your past.

Come Back

Suggested Reading:

Jann Howell's website **South Carolina Animal Psychic**

Great-Grandpa's in the Litter Box Dan Greenburg

Unfinished Business: What the Dead Can Teach Us About Life James Van Praagh

Repetition: Past Lives, Life, and Rebirth Doris Eliana Cohen, Ph.D.

Divine Guidance: How to Have a Dialogue with God and Your Guardian Angels Doreen Virtue, Ph.D.

Straight from the Horse's Mouth: How to Talk to Animals and Get Answers Amelia Kinkade

Suggested Listening:

Past Life Regression with the Angels Doreen Virtue, Ph.D.

Regression Through the Mirrors of Time Brian L. Weiss, M.D.

Regression to Times and Places Brian L. Weiss, M.D.

Spiritual Progress Through Regression Brian L. Weiss, M.D.

Tina Proffitt

About the Author

Tina Proffitt is the author of ten romance novels, mother to two life-long home-schooled teenagers, and wife to her best friend.

She holds a degree in education from the University of South Carolina and loves to read all things medieval, mysterious, and mystical.

She can be reached at her **website.** *Tina Proffitt: Small-town Southern Romance with a Mystical Side*

tinaproffitt.wordpress.com

Blogger: *Recipes from a Writer*

Goodreads

Pinterest

Facebook: Tina Proffitt Author Page

Twitter: @tina_proffitt

Instagram: tina_proffitt

Kitty and Juliet are pictured on the front cover, in our back yard, the day we brought Juliet home.

Come Back

Novels by Tina Proffitt:

First Forever: Fredericksburg County Series Book 1
Second Chances: Fredericksburg County Series Book 2
Third Time's the Charm: Fredericksburg County Series Book 3
A Sprinkle of Magick
Shadow Walker
Parlor Favors
The Almoner's Tale
Red Nobody
Ten for a Bird
Event Horizon: Chances Are Series Book 1